Number 129
Spring 2011

New Directions for Evaluation

Sandra Mathison
Editor-in-Chief

Multisite Evaluation Practice: Lessons and Reflections From Four Cases

Jean A. King
Frances Lawrenz
Editors

MULTISITE EVALUATION PRACTICE: LESSONS AND REFLECTIONS FROM
FOUR CASES
Jean A. King, Frances Lawrenz (eds.)
New Directions for Evaluation, no. 129
Sandra Mathison, Editor-in-Chief

Microfilm copies of issues and articles are available in 16mm and 35mm, as well as microfiche in 105mm, through University Microfilms Inc., 300 North Zeeb Road, Ann Arbor, MI 48106-1346.

New Directions for Evaluation is indexed in Cambridge Scientific Abstracts (CSA/CIG), Contents Pages in Education (T & F), Higher Education Abstracts (Claremont Graduate University), Social Services Abstracts (CSA/CIG), Sociological Abstracts (CSA/CIG), and Worldwide Political Sciences Abstracts (CSA/CIG).

NEW DIRECTIONS FOR EVALUATION (ISSN 1097-6736, electronic ISSN 1534-875X) is part of The Jossey-Bass Education Series and is published quarterly by Wiley Subscription Services, Inc., A Wiley Company, at Jossey-Bass, 989 Market Street, San Francisco, CA 94103-1741.

SUBSCRIPTIONS cost $89 for U.S./Canada/Mexico; $113 international. For institutions, agencies, and libraries, $271 U.S.; $311 Canada/Mexico; $345 international. Prices subject to change.

EDITORIAL CORRESPONDENCE should be addressed to the Editor-in-Chief, Sandra Mathison, University of British Columbia, 2125 Main Mall, Vancouver, BC V6T 1Z4, Canada.

www.josseybass.com

Editorial Policy and Procedures

New Directions for Evaluation, a quarterly sourcebook, is an official publication of the American Evaluation Association. The journal publishes empirical, methodological, and theoretical works on all aspects of evaluation. A reflective approach to evaluation is an essential strand to be woven through every issue. The editors encourage issues that have one of three foci: (1) craft issues that present approaches, methods, or techniques that can be applied in evaluation practice, such as the use of templates, case studies, or survey research; (2) professional issues that present topics of import for the field of evaluation, such as utilization of evaluation or locus of evaluation capacity; (3) societal issues that draw out the implications of intellectual, social, or cultural developments for the field of evaluation, such as the women's movement, communitarianism, or multiculturalism. A wide range of substantive domains is appropriate for *New Directions for Evaluation;* however, the domains must be of interest to a large audience within the field of evaluation. We encourage a diversity of perspectives and experiences within each issue, as well as creative bridges between evaluation and other sectors of our collective lives.

The editors do not consider or publish unsolicited single manuscripts. Each issue of the journal is devoted to a single topic, with contributions solicited, organized, reviewed, and edited by a guest editor. Issues may take any of several forms, such as a series of related chapters, a debate, or a long article followed by brief critical commentaries. In all cases, the proposals must follow a specific format, which can be obtained from the editor-in-chief. These proposals are sent to members of the editorial board and to relevant substantive experts for peer review. The process may result in acceptance, a recommendation to revise and resubmit, or rejection. However, the editors are committed to working constructively with potential guest editors to help them develop acceptable proposals.

Sandra Mathison, Editor-in-Chief
University of British Columbia
2125 Main Mall
Vancouver, BC V6T 1Z4
CANADA
e-mail: nde@eval.org

CONTENTS

Editors' Notes

The Beyond Evaluation Use research project started as a synergistic collaboration between two long-time colleagues, one of whom works in small, local settings where participatory evaluation is often a financial necessity, and the other of whom regularly engages in large-scale, federally funded evaluations. One of us has a humanities background and is primarily qualitative in orientation; the other has a background in the sciences and is more quantitative in orientation. As we have worked together over the years, we have uncovered many other areas of difference, but the one topic on which our interests have always converged emphatically was the question of how to increase the value of the evaluation processes we direct and the products that our evaluations generate. Thus was born a research project to address the question of to what extent participation in multisite program evaluations affects the people who are leading or evaluating projects being evaluated by their funder.

Here was our reasoning. The field already understands the importance of engaging primary intended users (Patton, 2008), and research has shown that by doing so, we can increase the likelihood of use (Cousins, 2003; Johnson et al., 2009). But multisite evaluations are different from the single settings where scholars have most typically conducted research on evaluation use. In multisite settings where projects are funded, for example, by a government agency at any level or by a large national or international foundation, there is another important group in addition to the primary intended users at the funding agency: the leaders of the local funded projects. If each of the funded project sites is expected to take part in or support the overall program evaluation, then staff at those sites must in some way do something for the evaluation; in our experience the project leaders and local evaluators frequently serve as the link between their individual project and the larger cross-project evaluation of the funded program.

Despite their importance, the field had not yet addressed the topic of how being asked or required to participate in such evaluations affects these individuals who play a critical role in multisite evaluations. These are the liaisons to the organizations implementing the program at different sites. With them, multisite evaluators have a contact in each project who can facilitate and trouble shoot the multisite evaluation, ensuring a sufficient quantity of high-quality data; without them, multisite evaluators may find themselves on their own trying to generate or compile accurate information, a huge challenge when there are multiple projects at geographically diverse locations. This research, then, is not about primary intended users, but rather about secondary, possibly unintended users who participate in the evaluation either by choice or requirement, but who may hold the fate of

New Directions for Evaluation, no. 129, Spring 2011 © Wiley Periodicals, Inc., and the American Evaluation Association. Published online in Wiley Online Library (wileyonlinelibrary.com) • DOI: 10.1002/ev.348

the larger evaluation in their hands. The importance of the research stems from the increasing numbers of large, multisite studies and the amount of funding spent on them, along with the potential value gained or lost when project staff provide or fail to provide support to the evaluation process.

Based on two ever-lengthening careers that include growing numbers of evaluations, our assumption always was that these potential secondary users—the project principal investigators (PIs) and evaluators—probably did get something from helping with the program evaluation. The concepts of participatory evaluation (Burke, 1998; King, 2007), process use (Cousins, 2007; Lawrenz, Huffman, & McGinnis, 2007; Patton, 2008), and evaluation use more generally (Cousins, 2003; Johnson et al., 2009) support such an assumption, and we wanted to see if that assumption was correct. So, although the National Science Foundation (NSF) was the primary user and client in each of the program evaluations we studied, the research team did not examine NSF's use of the evaluation process or findings, but rather focused on the local project staff. We wanted to study the differences that might arise when people were, on the one hand, required to engage in evaluation activities specified by someone else (that is, the program evaluator working for the funder) or, on the other hand, were actively involved in making decisions about how to conduct the larger study.

As already noted, one of our grounding concepts was the research that has examined the effects of participation in evaluation on the use of evaluation processes and findings. As also noted, however, these cases were not about participatory evaluation as commonly understood (that is, an evaluation in a single place or with a finite group of people). Instead, this research addressed large multisite evaluations where the "participants" were not individuals, but rather individual projects, each implementing a different approach at its unique site (Lawrenz & Huffman, 2003). Therefore, the study collected data from individual people who served as representatives of their respective projects. To highlight this distinction, we used the term *involvement* rather than *participation* (Toal, 2009; Toal, King, Johnson, & Lawrenz, 2008). Our initial assumption was that individuals from projects who were more actively involved would be more likely to use the results of the program evaluation.

In addition, we also wanted to study the effects of multisite evaluations on another group of people: the opinion leaders of a field more generally. We wanted to see if or to what extent a large-scale multisite evaluation might also make a difference more broadly, regardless of whether the national program evaluators were instructed to consider project and field use in their evaluation design. The concept of evaluation influence has celebrated its tenth birthday, but there is currently little formal research about the effects of multisite evaluations on specific content areas (for example, to what extent individual studies have influenced a field like science, technology, engineering, and mathematics [STEM] education) or on program evaluation (for example, to what extent individual studies have influenced

NEW DIRECTIONS FOR EVALUATION • DOI: 10.1002/ev

general evaluation practice). In this sense, we also considered people representing broad fields as potential users to trace the influence of evaluation studies.

This, then, is the new direction that this issue of *New Directions* will address. We applied the overarching issues of involvement and evaluation use/influence in framing the study, and its findings are novel in that they introduce the study of involvement and use by secondary intended users or perhaps even *unintended* users. The cases presented in this issue represent four NSF-funded educational programs and associated evaluations spanning 15 years (1993–2008) and many national changes (see Figure 1.1). The four case studies, analyses, and cross-case synthesis that form the first six chapters were produced as part of the "Beyond Evaluation Use" research project funded by the National Science Foundation (NSF) from 2004–2008. We are extremely aware and want to state clearly that one of the researchers (Frances Lawrenz) had a role in each of the four evaluations we studied. We have worked hard to balance her insider knowledge and possible bias with the outside perspectives and objectivity of the rest of our research team, which included the following individuals (in chronological order): Ann Ooms, Laura Gorny, Linda Bosma, Delia Kundin, Lija Greenseid, Boris Volkov, Stacie Toal, Kelli Johnson, Denise Roseland, Gina Johnson, and Patricia Ross.

Data for the study were collected through multiple and mixed methods, including archival review, several surveys, interviews, and citation analyses.

Archival Review

We reviewed archival documents, publications, and reports produced by the program evaluations. In addition, the research team examined NSF publications summarizing program activities and identifying grantees, project reports published by individual projects and centers, evaluation instruments and handbooks, and articles published in scholarly journals based on the evaluations and on individual project-level activities.

Surveys

An on-line survey was distributed to 935 project primary investigators, coprimary investigators, coordinators, directors, administrators (that is, project leaders), and evaluators connected to the program evaluations. The number of project leaders and evaluators with valid e-mail addresses was 810, with an overall response rate of 46% (372/810). A nonrespondent survey showed no significant difference in the overall level of involvement reported. However, a significant difference was found between respondents and nonrespondents in the ATE and CETP programs with respect to the impact of the evaluations. In both cases, respondents reported higher levels

Figure 1.1. Timeline and Historical Grounding for the NSF Cases

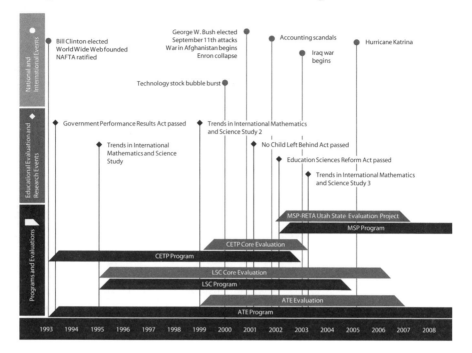

of impact than nonrespondents. In-depth interviews were conducted with two purposefully selected samples of project leaders and evaluators who responded to the survey. One sample contained respondents with varying reported levels of involvement and use, for example, low use–high involvement, whereas the other sample was entirely high users.

A second on-line survey of NSF PIs was administered to a sample of 350 individuals randomly selected from the database of over 2,000 currently funded NSF Education and Human Development Directorate PIs. The survey elicited responses about PIs' perceptions of evaluations, people, and publications that might have been influential on the fields of STEM evaluation and education. The overall response rate was 54% (191/349).

Interviews

Thirty-one interviews were conducted, with roughly eight interviews per evaluation. Interviews lasted between 30 and 50 minutes, and all were taped and transcribed. The interviews followed a standardized, semistructured protocol with flexibility in probing for additional details and description as necessary. In addition, one of the PIs conducted interviews with four NSF program officers who were partially responsible for at least one of the evaluations. In one additional form of "interview," the four evaluators who directed the evaluations provided in-depth reflections on their experiences through written exercises, two advisory committee meetings, and a day-long retreat. The evaluators were asked to reflect on the intended and actual levels of individual project involvement in their evaluations and how the individual projects and others used the program evaluation findings and processes. In a second additional form of "interview," a very brief e-mail/telephone survey of editors/coeditors of six journals in the evaluation and STEM education fields was conducted. This inquiry sought to determine if the editors were aware of any articles that had been published about influential STEM evaluations. Responses were obtained from three of six editors or coeditors.

Citation Analysis

With the use of a complete list of all publications, presentations, and instruments (that is, "evaluation products") developed by the three program evaluations, a citation analysis was conducted to analyze patterns of influence the evaluations had on the fields of STEM education and evaluation. The citation databases Web of Science and Google Scholar and the Google search engine were used to identify 376 citations to the 246 evaluation products. The citations and products were coded based on their type, field, and author to allow for quantitative and visual analysis of the influence networks of products and citations.

The Structure of This Issue

The current issue has two sections. The first section (Chapters 1–6) contains the NSF multisite case data and related analyses, responding to the research questions concerning the patterns of involvement in large, multisite evaluation projects and the extent to which different levels of involvement in program evaluations resulted in different patterns of evaluation use and influence. Chapters 1–4 provide summaries of longer case studies describing the documented involvement and use of participants in four NSF evaluation projects that had differing levels of involvement: program-level evaluations of three NSF programs (Advanced Technological Education, Collaboratives for Excellence in Teacher Preparation, and Local Systemic Change through Teacher Enhancement), and one evaluation technical assistance project (the Math Science Partnership–Research, Evaluation and Technical Assistance Project at Utah State University) (Greenseid et al., 2009; Johnson et al., 2009; Roseland et al., 2009; Toal et al., 2009). Three of the four evaluation efforts would be considered traditional program evaluations, whereas the fourth, the MSP-RETA project, represented a program-level evaluation initiative that did not actually evaluate all of the projects, but instead was intended to provide evaluation technical assistance to them. Chapter 5 details the results of our study of the influence of the four evaluations, and Chapter 6 presents the results of a cross-case analysis.

This issue's second section offers reflections on the results of the NSF research, some by people who were part of the process and some by those who were not. The section content encourages readers to think about the implications of the research to improve the practice of multisite evaluation. Modeled after Alkin (1990), Chapter 7 contains themes and excerpts—lessons learned—from an edited transcript of a conversation among the four evaluators whose multisite evaluations were profiled in the case studies. Karen E. Kirkhart, a member of the research Advisory Committee, offers her perspective on critical cultural issues for multisite evaluations in Chapter 8. Chapter 9 gives the reflections of Paul R. Brandon, a scholar who is well versed in the research on evaluation participation and use, but who provides an external view of the case results. In Chapter 10, Leslie K. Goodyear describes her experiences leading another multisite evaluation that successfully engaged participants actively in the process through networking and dissemination, documenting effective practices for doing so. The final chapter (Chapter 11), written by another member of the research Advisory Committee, Melvin M. Mark, points to thoughts for future research on evaluation influence, especially in multisite settings.

We end these introductory notes by recording a key lesson gained after several years of research: Evaluators who want to make the most of multisite evaluations should think carefully not only about their primary intended users (which they should), but also about communicating with and, to the extent possible, involving secondary users, the staff, in funded projects. Doing so holds the potential to increase the eventual use and possibly the ultimate influence of the evaluation, surely a worthwhile goal.

References

Alkin, M. C. (1990). *Debates on evaluation*. Newbury Park, CA: Sage.

Burke, B. (1998). Evaluating for a change: Reflections on participatory methodology. *New Directions for Evaluation, 80*, 43–56.

Cousins, J. B. (2003). Utilization effects of participatory evaluation. In T. Kellaghan & D. L. Stufflebeam (Eds.), *International handbook of educational evaluation* (pp. 245–268). Boston: Kluwer Academic.

Cousins, J. B. (Ed.). (2007). Process use in theory, research, and practice. *New Directions for Evaluation, 116*.

Greenseid, L., Lawrenz, F., King, J. A., Johnson, G., Johnson, K., Ooms, A., & Volkov, B. (2009). *University of Minnesota Beyond Evaluation Use Project Report 3: A case study of involvement, use, and influence within the Collaboratives for Excellence in Teacher Preparation (CETP) Core Evaluation*. Minneapolis: University of Minnesota. Retrieved from http://www.cehd.umn.edu/projects/beu/documents.html

Johnson, K., Greenseid, L. O., Toal, S. A., King, J. A., Lawrenz, F., & Volkov, B. (2009). Research on evaluation use: A review of the empirical literature from 1986 to 2005. *American Journal of Evaluation, 30*(3), 377–410.

Johnson, K., Lawrenz, F., King, J. A., Greenseid, L., Johnson, G., Ooms, A., & Volkov, B. (2009). *University of Minnesota Beyond Evaluation Use Project Report 4: A case study* of the impact of the Local Systemic Change through Teacher Enhancement (LSC) Core Evaluation. Minneapolis: University of Minnesota. Retrieved from http://www.cehd .umn.edu/projects/beu/documents.html

King, J. A. (2007). Making sense of participatory evaluation: Framing participatory evaluation. New Directions for Evaluation, 114, 83–86.

Lawrenz, F., & Huffman, D. (2003). How can multi-site evaluations be participatory? American Journal of Evaluation, 24(4), 471–482.

Lawrenz, F., Huffman, D., & McGinnis, J. R. (2007). Multi-level evaluation process use in large scale multi-site evaluation. New Directions for Evaluation, 116, 75–85.

Patton, M. Q. (2008). Utilization-focused evaluation (4th ed.). Thousand Oaks, CA: Sage.

Roseland, D., Volkov, B., Lawrenz, F., King, J. A., Greenseid, L., Johnson, G., & Toal, S. (2009). University of Minnesota Beyond Evaluation Use Project Report 5: A case study of the impact and involvement of the Utah State Math Science Partnership (MSP)–Research, Evaluation, and Technical Assistance (RETA) Project. Minneapolis: University of Minnesota. Retrieved from http://www.cehd.umn.edu/projects/beu/documents.html

Toal, S., Lawrenz, F., King, J. A., Greenseid, L., Johnson, G., Johnson, K., & Volkov, B. (2009). University of Minnesota Beyond Evaluation Use Project Report 2: A case study of the impact of the Advanced Technological Education (ATE) Program Evaluation. Minneapolis: University of Minnesota. Retrieved from http://www.cehd.umn.edu /projects/beu/documents.html

Toal, S. A. (2009). The validation of the evaluation involvement scale for use in multi-site settings. American Journal of Evaluation, 30(3), 349–362.

Toal, S. A., King, J. A., Johnson, K., & Lawrenz, F. (2008). The unique character of involvement in multi-site evaluation settings. Evaluation and Program Planning, 32(2), 91–98.

Jean A. King
Frances Lawrenz
Editors

JEAN A. KING is a professor and director of graduate studies in the Department of Organizational Leadership, Policy, and Development at the University of Minnesota.

FRANCES LAWRENZ is the Wallace Professor of Teaching and Learning in the Department of Educational Psychology and the associate vice president for research at the University of Minnesota.

NEW DIRECTIONS FOR EVALUATION • DOI: 10.1002/ev

Toal, S. A., & Gullickson, A. R. (2011). The upside of an annual survey in light of involvement and use: Evaluating the Advanced Technological Education program. In J. A. King & F. Lawrenz (Eds.), *Multisite evaluation practice: Lessons and reflections from four cases. New Directions for Evaluation, 129*, 9–15.

1

The Upside of an Annual Survey in Light of Involvement and Use: Evaluating the Advanced Technological Education Program

Stacie A. Toal, Arlen R. Gullickson

Abstract

In 1999, the National Science Foundation (NSF) awarded funds to the Evaluation Center at Western Michigan University to conduct an external evaluation of the Advanced Technological Education (ATE) program. ATE, a federally mandated program designed to increase the number and quality of skilled technicians in the U.S. workforce, has funded over 346 projects and centers across the nation. This case study describes the relationship between project-level involvement in the ATE program evaluation and the use and influence of the evaluation on project primary investigators and evaluators. Although this large, multisite program evaluation employed numerous evaluative data-collection and dissemination techniques, project leaders and evaluators associated the program evaluation primarily with an annual Web-based survey. The NSF's expectation that projects would complete the annual survey contributed to feelings of involvement and, in many cases, promoted use and impact. © Wiley Periodicals, Inc., and the American Evaluation Association.

W orking under a Congressional mandate, the National Science Foundation (NSF) created the Advanced Technological Education (ATE) program in 1992 to improve technological education. The NSF aimed to increase the number and quality of skilled technicians in the workforce, thus improving U.S. competitiveness amidst growing global competition. Viewed as a conduit for preparing technicians, community colleges received most of the ATE funds to strengthen scientific/technical education and training capabilities in biotechnology, environmental technology, global information systems (GIS), manufacturing, and telecommunications.

This Congressional charge resulted in a large diversity of high-budget projects and centers. For example, between 1994 and 2005, the ATE program funded 674 projects and centers, making grants to 345 unique institutions of which more than 200 were 2-year colleges. The cost of the program totaled approximately $350 million. The ATE program funded large Centers of Excellence (up to $5 million for 4 years) and smaller-scale projects (up to $300,000 for 3 years). ATE projects focused on improving technical education materials, enhancing technical instruction, and providing professional development to faculty and teachers. Grantees established partnerships with high schools, 2- and 4-year colleges, businesses, government agencies, and professional societies to improve the nation's advanced technology workforce.

ATE Evaluation Background

The diversity of ATE projects in terms of scope, stakeholders, organizations, and project or center practices created unique challenges to understanding program-level effectiveness. Nevertheless, NSF remained committed to both project-level and program-level evaluation. Therefore, in 1999 NSF funded the Evaluation Center at Western Michigan University (WMU) to conduct an external evaluation of the entire ATE program. The evaluation budget was appropriately large. Arlen R. Gullickson, principal investigator (PI), received two consecutive NSF grants: an initial grant of $1.3 million covered 1999–2002, and a subsequent grant of $1.8 million covered 2002–2006. Although some components of the ATE program evaluation (primarily the annual Web-based survey) and the ATE program itself are still ongoing, the scope of this case study is limited to the years 1999–2005. Consequently, ATE program and evaluation activities that have occurred since 2005 are neither considered nor commented upon, despite their potential impact on involvement and use/influence.

The WMU evaluation focused on program-wide productivity, with the primary audience being NSF staff. It is important to understand that the evaluators structured the evaluation in a manner that would allow them to provide feedback to NSF, so that NSF could use the evaluation information for programmatic decisions and accountability reports to Congress. Consequently, the evaluation was not intentionally designed to influence the projects and centers. With that said, program-level feedback was regularly disseminated to projects in hopes of improving project-level processes and outcomes.

Principal evaluation activities included collecting descriptive data, developing an annual Web-based evaluation survey to collect data over time, conducting site visits, drafting targeted reports on various aspects of the program, and providing formative evaluation information to NSF staff and to the projects and centers. The annual Web-based surveys collected primarily quantitative, but also some qualitative data on the activities, accomplishments, and effectiveness of ATE projects and centers for general accountability purposes. The series of 13 extensive site visits to centers and projects validated and illuminated survey findings and allowed evaluators to gather detailed information about project operations and outcomes. The sites were selected with the use of a purposive sampling technique based on survey data and NSF program officer input to be representative of the diversity of the ATE projects. Teams of trained site visitors included evaluators, industry representatives, and education experts. Finally, the evaluators conducted four targeted studies on different program components: (a) the value added by ATE projects and centers to business and industry, (b) the development of materials for ATE project use, (c) the professional development provided by the ATE projects, and (d) the sustainability of ATE projects' impacts.

In terms of involvement in the evaluation process, the process of creating the survey framework and the question wording engaged NSF program officers and an evaluation advisory group. The evaluation advisory group, comprised of individuals who worked directly with ATE projects and centers, helped conceptualize the survey and contributed to item development. Individual ATE grantees had relatively little participation or input, primarily because the evaluation focused more on NSF's needs, not on the needs of individual funded projects.

Method

This chapter presents empirical data to describe what involvement in the program evaluation activities meant to project staff and their subsequent use and influence of the evaluation process and findings. Data for this research were collected through five distinct sources of information:

- An on-line survey of ATE project leaders and evaluators about their involvement in and use of the ATE program evaluation ($n = 188/409$, 46% response rate). This survey should not be confused with the program evaluation's annual Web-based survey.
- Follow-up interviews of ATE project leaders and evaluators ($n = 9$) who also responded to the on-line survey on involvement and use.
- An interview with one of multiple NSF program officers responsible for the ATE program at the time.
- Review of archival documents, publications, and reports produced by the ATE program and the program evaluation.
- Reflections provided by the ATE program evaluation principal investigator Arlen R. Gullickson, a coauthor of this chapter.

Findings

Involvement

Results from the survey respondents and interviews suggest that, overall, involvement in the program evaluation was generally low to moderate, centering primarily on the annual Web-based survey that was expected of all projects by their second year of funding. For example, survey respondents reported at least a little involvement in all stages of the evaluation, such as discussions that focused on planning the evaluation, data collection and interpretation, and communication of the results. Means in each of the 13 activities ranged from 2.2 to 2.7 on a 4-point scale (1 = *none*, 2 = *yes, a little*, 3 = *yes, some*, 4 = *extensively*); however, each activity had at least one-third of respondents reporting that they were not at all involved (37.1–47.7%). The means and percentages for each activity showed little variation, perhaps a reflection of the evaluator-directed program evaluation. The interview data supported the survey results related to low to moderate feelings of involvement. When asked about the ways in which they were involved in the program evaluation (if any), all of the interviewees mentioned completing the annual Web-based survey. However, the submission of the survey by itself did not engender feelings of involvement. For example, one PI explained that she had no involvement in the program evaluation except for filling out the survey, which she did only because she felt it was required. Consequently, the PI qualified her level of involvement as only "a little."

Results from the interviews also suggested that perceptions of involvement appeared to be stronger for interviewees who also provided input on question development or were asked to make a presentation at a meeting. Almost all interviewees mentioned attendance at annual meetings as involvement. It is interesting to note that attendance or participation at the annual meetings did not typically include any activities related to the program evaluation. One interviewee explained that she completed a questionnaire about the program evaluation (response to questions, timing, and so on) during the annual conference; however, the other interviewees' experiences only indirectly related to the evaluation. Other involvement reported by the interviewees included volunteering to pilot test or to serve on a committee and studying or reporting results to others. Overall, respondents who reported higher levels of involvement seemed to interact more with the program evaluation, its staff, and the data collection associated with the annual Web-based survey from the program evaluators.

Use by Project PIs and Evaluators

Somewhat surprisingly, the reported levels of involvement did not translate into equally low levels of use. In general, results from the survey and the interviews suggest that the evaluation did affect project leaders and evaluators, in some cases extensively. Despite the fact that means for each area of use never exceeded 2.7 on a 4.0 scale, as was the case with the involvement questions, there were more use items on the survey that had means of 2.6 and 2.7, whereas the involvement items hovered more around 2.1 and 2.2. In addition, interviewees provided more examples of use than of involvement. Despite the tedium and time often associated with the annual Web-based survey, the majority of interviewees acknowledged that completing the annual Web-based survey for the program evaluation was, in general, useful and had an impact on their projects. Interviewees offered specific examples of use and influence such as:

> "It helped me to figure out how to evaluate the program."
> "We [the project] look at it [the survey] to see how to move ahead."
> "I am working with so many groups and that tended to keep me focused on what I was doing rather than looking beyond. So, I really felt that when I went to the survey and went to the evaluation groups that it gave me a broader perspective."
> "I would say that I definitely learned some new evaluation skills."

Survey results indicated that the highest percentages of extensive use were related to beliefs about the planning, implementation, and communication stages of an evaluation (as opposed to knowledge or skills). For those survey respondents who participated in another evaluation after the ATE program evaluations, over 80% reported using what they learned from planning and implementing the evaluation in another context. Survey results suggested that even the least-used aspect of the evaluation, the data-collection instruments, were used to at least a small extent by over 60% of the respondents.

Survey respondents and interviewees were asked to identify factors that may have either limited or enabled use. The most common limitation related to a lack of resources, either in terms of time or personnel. In addition, the generality due to the broad, national scope of the program evaluation created a feeling among some project staff that their project was not being represented favorably or meaningfully. Limitations aside, both survey and interview respondents mentioned that collaboration with other projects fostered by the program evaluation elicited gratitude and in many cases seemed to initiate use. Results indicated that the evaluation also increased awareness among project leaders and evaluators about the extent to which their project was meeting its goals. Interviewees explained that increased collaboration and awareness sparked ideas for project improvements.

Implications of an "Expected" Annual Survey

As previously mentioned, the ATE program evaluation had several components beyond the most central feature, the annual Web-based survey. The evaluation team disseminated results from all of the activities by a variety of mechanisms, both traditional and creative, in an effort to promote use.

However, in terms of involvement and use, survey respondents and interviewees seemed to associate the program evaluation almost exclusively with the annual Web-based survey.

So, the question remains: Why did projects focus almost exclusively on the annual survey instead of the numerous other activities whose results were disseminated? The answer may be twofold. First, the annual Web-based survey was requested and expected of all of the projects, not just a few selected projects, as was the case with the site visits. It seems equally important that, despite it not being required of grantees, the clear expectation of survey completion by the WMU evaluation team and the NSF after the first year of funding created a strong impetus for projects to complete it. In fact, the NSF program officers asked the evaluation team to report names of persons who did not respond to the survey. This pressure proved to be an effective "big stick."

Although project leaders and evaluators were most likely to report that their engagement in all of the stages of the program evaluation (planning, implementation, and communication) had been voluntary, a sizeable group (32–38%) also reported that they felt involvement was required. Survey respondents were most likely to report feeling required to be involved in the final stage of the evaluation: communication of the findings. This finding is possibly a reflection of the type of data required by the annual Web-based survey: detailed reporting of the project's activities, especially in terms of the numbers of people served, activities, hours, etc. Project staff likely could have felt that communication of findings was required if they considered completing the annual Web-based survey a way of communicating their own project's performance and activities.

PIs and evaluators also acknowledged during the interviews that they felt as if the survey was required and/or part of their responsibility. One PI explained that she felt that the learning about other projects and sharing details of her own was part of her responsibility to the program:

> It's part of our responsibility. We're working within this grant and we need to be able to go out and share information with other people and learn things from other people so that we can make sure that our program is doing what it needs to do and get ideas to make it better and to be able to share what we've learned with other people.

Beyond the responsibility aspect, another PI offered that she felt the sharing provided some benefit to her project. She explained, "I'm pretty proud of the work we've done here and the progress we've made, and so it was nice to be able to fill out a survey that got some other recognition." However, the reported involvement and use was not always perceived as positive, especially if the content of questions was not aligned well with project activities and processes. The more positive perceptions of involvement and use were associated with additional experiences either related to the

NEW DIRECTIONS FOR EVALUATION • DOI: 10.1002/ev

survey development (piloting questions, reviewing drafts, presenting at annual meetings) or the opportunity to promote or share positive project-level data as a result of the survey.

Given the goals of this national evaluation—to provide details on program-wide productivity and accountability to the NSF and Congress—the annual Web-based survey alone would not have adequately captured project-level activities. Consequently, the additional activities were critical to the evaluation, despite having a reportedly minimal impact on creating feelings of project involvement and project-level use. In summary, by creating a clear expectation that the annual survey be completed, the evaluators successfully pushed projects to complete the survey, which in turn generated feelings of involvement for many and promoted use of the results.

STACIE A. TOAL is the principal of Cannon River Consulting, located in Northfield, Minnesota; she completed her Ph.D. in the Department of Educational Policy and Administration at the University of Minnesota.

ARLEN R. GULLICKSON is an emeritus professor at Western Michigan University (WMU) and director of Evalua|t|e, an NSF-funded evaluation resource center housed in The Evaluation Center at WMU for the Advanced Technological Education Program.

Johnson, K., & Weiss, I. R. (2011). Compulsory project-level involvement and the use of program-level evaluations: Evaluating the Local Systemic Change for Teacher Enhancement program. In J. A. King & F. Lawrenz (Eds.), *Multisite evaluation practice: Lessons and reflections from four cases*. New Directions for Evaluation, 129, 17–23.

2

Compulsory Project-Level Involvement and the Use of Program-Level Evaluations: Evaluating the Local Systemic Change for Teacher Enhancement Program

Kelli Johnson, Iris R. Weiss

Abstract

In 1995, the National Science Foundation (NSF) contracted with principal investigator Iris Weiss and an evaluation team at Horizon Research, Inc. (HRI) to conduct a national evaluation of the Local Systemic Change for Teacher Enhancement program (LSC). HRI conducted the core evaluation under a $6.25 million contract with NSF. This program evaluation project, called the LSC core evaluation, had an overarching program-wide focus that included all 88 local LSC projects. The LSC core evaluation was a large, multisite program evaluation that included multiple data-collection and information-dissemination activities. Each local LSC project was required to have a project-level evaluator, to collect information by using predesigned data-collection instruments developed by HRI, and to report findings to the core evaluation on a regular basis. This case study describes the relationship between project-level involvement in the LSC core evaluation and the use of the core evaluation by project leaders and evaluators. © Wiley Periodicals Inc., and the American Evaluation Association.

New Directions for Evaluation, no. 129, Spring 2011 © Wiley Periodicals, Inc., and the American Evaluation Association. Published online in Wiley Online Library (wileyonlinelibrary.com) • DOI: 10.1002/ev.350

17

A $250 million program that spanned the decade 1995–2005, the Local Systemic Change for Teacher Enhancement program (LSC), funded 88 projects and eventually reached 4,000 schools in 31 states and 476 districts. The program targeted K–12 teachers, requiring a minimum of 130 hours of professional development to prepare them to implement district-designated instructional materials. The NSF created the LSC program to provide high-quality professional development to teachers across entire school districts to enhance math, science, and technology education. The LSC program was based on the idea that district-wide professional development for teachers would deepen their content knowledge, provide support among colleagues for teaching according to national standards, and ultimately lead to higher student achievement. LSC professional development often consisted of multiweek summer institutes, with follow-up support offered to teachers throughout the school year.

LSC Evaluation Background

Iris Weiss and the core-evaluation team at Horizon Research, Inc. in Chapel Hill, North Carolina began their work on the LSC core evaluation under a contract with NSF in 1995. The core evaluation was intended to assess the status of individual LSC projects, as well as to collect information that could be aggregated to inform broader messages to the NSF, Congress, and the public. Each of the 88 local LSC projects was required to gather specific information with the use of evaluation instruments designed by HRI; in addition to the required elements, projects were allowed to add their own evaluation components.

The core evaluation required each local project to follow specific data-collection protocols. Explicitly, they had to observe both professional development and classroom sessions, administer questionnaires to teachers and principals in all participating schools, and conduct interviews with teachers and members of the projects' administrative teams. The local evaluators were required to conduct analyses, form their own judgments, and then submit a summary analytic report to HRI. These evaluators were also required to participate in annual meetings that provided orientation and training on the use of the standardized data-collection instruments, as well as special training on the classroom-observation protocols that included observing and rating videotaped classroom lessons.

In terms of involvement in the evaluation design, after the first few years, individual projects had little input. However, the core-evaluation team did consult extensively with the projects that were in place at the beginning of the core evaluation regarding the adequacy of the evaluation design and the data-collection instruments. In addition, as the need for modifications to the core evaluation became apparent over time, there were multiple opportunities for local project leaders and evaluators to offer their input.

NEW DIRECTIONS FOR EVALUATION • DOI: 10.1002/ev

Method

The overall purpose of the LSC core evaluation was to assess the status of individual projects in a way that yielded data that could be aggregated across the program nationwide for the NSF's use. The research study described in this chapter gathered empirical data to describe what involvement in the core-evaluation activities meant to the projects and to describe the subsequent use of the evaluation process and findings on the projects. Data for this research were collected through an on-line survey of LSC project leaders and evaluators about their involvement in and use of the LSC program evaluation.

A total of 74 project leaders and evaluators completed the survey for an overall response rate of 53%. However, data provided by one respondent were unusable, thus reducing the total number of respondents to 73. Of the 73, 43 were LSC project leaders, and the remaining 30 were local evaluators. In addition to the on-line survey ($n = 73$), follow-up interviews were conducted with LSC project leaders and evaluators ($n = 7$) who responded to the survey and with a program officer from NSF involved with the LSC program at the time. Additional data were collected through review of archival documents, publications, and reports produced by the core evaluation, and reflections from the principal investigator (PI) of the core evaluation.

Findings

Involvement

Survey respondents reported moderate levels of involvement, with an overall involvement mean of 2.71 on a 4-point scale (1 = *none*; 2 = *yes, a little*; 3 = *yes, some*; 4 = *extensively*). The involvement measure had three components: planning, implementation, and communication. Involvement in planning had the lowest mean score at 2.4 on the 4-point scale. This result makes sense given the structure of the core evaluation, where only those LSC projects involved from the beginning of the LSC program had an opportunity to be involved in the evaluation planning.

Measures of the other two components of involvement—implementation and communication—showed differences in mean involvement levels between project leaders and evaluators. Not surprisingly, virtually all evaluators reported at least a little involvement in the implementation components (collecting, reviewing, analyzing, and interpreting data), with means ranging from 3.6 to 3.8. Many of the interviewees reported that they were involved in training, workshop attendance, and data-collection activities. Two of the three interviewees pointed to their involvement in data analysis and report writing, with one interviewee identifying that these two activities took place in the form of having to write an "analytic memo . . . in a format that Horizon gave us." With respect to involvement in the communications components (writing reports, reviewing reports, and presenting findings), nearly all evaluators said they had at least a little involvement, with a mean involvement level of 3.7 for evaluators and 2.0 for project PIs.

Overall, evaluators reported significantly higher levels of involvement than project leaders. The evaluators' mean involvement level was 3.0 compared to the project leaders' mean of 2.5 across all components of the overarching involvement measure. One evaluator who participated in a follow-up interview reported that she was involved in activity intended "to carry out whatever we were supposed to do for NSF—the teacher observations, the classroom and professional development observations, and other questions we had to address." Another evaluator noted in a follow-up interview that "we did what we were supposed to do and we went to the PI meetings," and a project PI noted that she ". . .was personally involved when they asked the PI to fill a form out. I always did that one."

Use by Project PIs and Evaluators

LSC evaluators and project leaders felt that their input to the core evaluation was considered and used. Over 95% reported that their input was considered at least a little overall, whereas more than 90% reported at least a little evaluation use during the planning, implementation, or communication stages. One interviewee reported, "I think they took it into consideration . . . I think Horizon was sensitive to massaging and adjusting the classroom observation protocol to reflect more of a constructive approach—an open-ended approach to science teaching." Another interviewee commented on feeling listened to by the core-evaluation staff. This interviewee touched on adjustments to the data-collection instruments that were discussed at the final meeting on the 10th anniversary. He said, "I don't know if it was my opinion that was taken into consideration or everybody's collective opinion. . . . [but] I felt a little bit of ownership because those were some of the comments I had offered." Data from the survey suggest that the LSC core evaluation had some perceived effect on the skills of project leaders and evaluators, with a mean level of influence of 2.89 on a 4-point scale (1 = none; 2 = yes, a little; 3 = yes, some; 4 = extensively). This same mean level of influence (2.89) was found for the effects on the knowledge and understanding of both project leaders and evaluators. Finally, the mean perceived effect on the beliefs of project leaders in the importance of STEM (Science, Technology, Engineering, and Mathematics) evaluation resulted in a mean level of 2.55 for evaluators and 2.85 for project leaders.

Several interviewees said they learned new evaluation skills as a result of the core evaluation. One interviewee cited having acquired new skills, namely "interview techniques, ways of documenting interviews, ways to . . . make similar judgments and use some of our coding across interviews . . ." Another interviewee commented on the way that the evaluation process affected interaction among LSC project staff, saying:

> In the initial 2 years if I said something, if it [was] going to impact the teach-
> ers, they were hesitant to use it. But . . . we took some of the teachers to PI
> meetings [and] I think it definitely made a difference, and they had better
> communication to be able to address some of these items.

A different interviewee described the importance of the paradigm-shifting insight relative to the change in thinking and beliefs about the value of activity in the education field. This interviewee noted:

> [W]e had the mentality that any inquiry or any hands-on activity was good.
> And so it was a nice way to start to think about that not all inquiry was good.
> It had to be high-quality inquiry, not just "activity for activity's sake." So, in
> the sense of looking at inquiry as hands-on activity, again, I think that [class-
> room observation] protocol impacted me personally.

Among those respondents who have conducted an evaluation since the LSC evaluation, about 90% of respondents reported that they used what they learned at least a little in another context. Approximately 70% of respondents reported having used the LSC program evaluation plan as a model for another evaluation, and 87% reported using the LSC data-collection instruments in another evaluation context. One of the interviewees described having used the classroom observation protocols in other settings:

> We used [them] quite extensively in the training of our lead teachers and in the
> lead teachers helping their peers. So, even though it was supposed to be—from
> the core evaluation's perspective—part of that core data collection, we ended up
> using it as a way of helping teachers understand what a good lesson looked like.

Enabling and Constraining Factors

The interviewees identified the quality and rigor of the instruments and the overall evaluation process as positive factors in lending credibility, and thus impact, to the core-evaluation products and activities. The interviewees provided more examples of barriers to influence than facilitators of influence. These barriers fell into three areas: (a) timing, (b) lack of alignment, and (c) information overload.

Interviewees commented that the timing of the core evaluation created more work and added costs to the local projects. Specifically, one interviewee noted that in planning their project-level evaluation, "no time was allocated for the national evaluation because it didn't exist at the time [the local evaluation was developed]." This project leader added that the core evaluation was "time put on top of what I needed to do. [It] impinged on the evaluation activities that I could do . . ."

Lack of alignment referred to the competing priorities between program and project evaluation activity. One of the interviewees described this constraint as follows:

> The external evaluation . . . used up a good deal of our degrees of freedom, probably known as social capital, with our teachers and administrators because it [the core evaluation] had to be assigned a priority position in terms of data collection. It then interfered with us being able to lay on a second level of data collection without putting undue demands on teachers and administrators and students. . . .[We] could only take so much time away from teaching and learning for data collection.

Finally, interviewees frequently mentioned information overload related to questions about their use of the core-evaluation reports. When asked about the extent to which the reports published by the core evaluation were used at the project level, interviewees often stated that they were unable to recall or that they had not been able to keep up with all of the information coming across their desks.

Implications

This case presents some of the effects of the core evaluation on individual project leaders' and evaluators' knowledge, skills, and beliefs, as well as on their future project activities. Several of the interviewees identified specific examples of the impact of their involvement in the core evaluation on themselves as well as on their projects. One interviewee commented that involvement in the core evaluation changed how he felt about the use of evaluation, saying:

> Basically I think it made us look more systematically. Had I just gone into classes and started observing about what's going on here, my observations would have been much more vague and less specific and less useful that way. I think in the fact of knowing that the data I was collecting was being done in [a] way to be compiled with other people's data . . . gave us a sense of the importance of what we were doing in serving on a national level and helped us get past the frustrations of not succeeding as well on the local level . . .

Another interviewee stressed that involvement in the core evaluation generated increased sensitivity to the diversity among projects and the associated diversity of data needs. This interviewee said:

> I became more sensitive to the complexity and difficulties in doing program-wide evaluations in terms of handling the uniqueness and the individual characteristics of projects within—I think there was nearly 100 different projects in the LSC program—I think I became more sensitive about that . . . [A]n instrument that might be impressive to a bunch of academic researchers may not have the same impact on a politician or policy maker. Therefore, we found that we had to supplement the project-wide data sources with unique things that reflected the [local] character . . .

Finally, one interviewee described the value of the core evaluation's meetings, noting that they ". . . established a network of people that you were able to call on later and as you faced difficulties and that's probably a critical thing." Overall, the findings are consistent with the idea that involvement in the evaluation activities was associated with the use of the evaluation in later projects and activities.

KELLI JOHNSON is a research fellow at the University of Minnesota School of Public Health and a doctoral candidate in the Department of Organizational Leadership, Policy and Development at the University of Minnesota.

IRIS R. WEISS is president of Horizon Research, Inc., a contract research firm in Chapel Hill, North Carolina, specializing in research and evaluation in science and mathematics education.

NEW DIRECTIONS FOR EVALUATION • DOI: 10.1002/ev

Greenseid, L. O., & Lawrenz, F. (2011). Tensions and trade-offs in voluntary involvement:
Evaluating the Collaboratives for Excellence in Teacher Preparation. In J. A. King &
F. Lawrenz (Eds.), *Multisite evaluation practice: Lessons and reflections from four cases.*
New Directions for Evaluation, 129, 25–31.

3

Tensions and Trade-Offs in Voluntary Involvement: Evaluating the Collaboratives for Excellence in Teacher Preparation

Lija O. Greenseid, Frances Lawrenz

Abstract

A team at the University of Minnesota conducted the Collaboratives for Excellence in Teacher Preparation (CETP) core evaluation between 1999 and 2004. The purpose of the CETP core evaluation was to achieve consensus among CETP project leaders and project evaluators on evaluation questions; to develop, pilot, and field test evaluation instruments tied to the questions; and to collect data to document the accomplishments of the CETP projects. This chapter examines the relationship between project-level involvement in the CETP core evaluation and the use of the evaluation by project principal investigators (PIs) and evaluators. The chapter examines the tensions and trade-offs that arose from attempting to balance voluntary involvement by project PIs and evaluators in the planning and development of the evaluation with the need to collect complete and comparable data across project sites. © Wiley Periodicals Inc., and the American Evaluation Association.

In the early 1990s, the National Science Foundation (NSF) responded to the national need for more well-qualified math and science teachers by creating the Collaboratives for Excellence in Teacher Preparation (CETP) program. CETP sought to improve teacher preparation by enhancing science, mathematics, and educational methods courses at the college level. The program also sought to increase collaboration within and between K–12 and higher-education institutions to foster the development of well-trained teachers competent in science and math. As its name indicates, collaboration was the hallmark of the CETP program. To be eligible, projects had to demonstrate institutional support and collaboration among 2-year, 4-year, and research institutions, school districts, the business community, and state departments of education. From 1993 to 2003, the NSF funded 19 CETPs, each involving from 3 to 15 higher-education institutions (including colleges, universities, and community colleges), as well as several school districts. Individual projects could apply for up to $1 million per year for 3–5 years. After the initial awards, CETPs could apply for three additional years of funding, in part to cover the costs of evaluation activities.

CETP Evaluation Background

Initially, the NSF required each newly funded CETP project to conduct its own project-level evaluation. These evaluations were predominantly formative in nature, intended to provide local project leaders with data to improve their project efforts. A summative evaluation effort was funded a year later to comply with governmental requirements to provide evidence of program impacts (Government Performance Results Act of 1993). In doing so, the NSF contracted with SRI International between 1994 and 1999 to conduct a summative evaluation of the first five CETP projects that were funded. The SRI evaluation employed a quasiexperimental design comparing the outcomes of higher-educational institutions involved in CETP projects with similar institutions not participating in the program. In the end, the SRI evaluation found few significant differences between the CETP projects and comparison groups because of small sample sizes and the study's being conducted at an early stage in the program's development. Consequently, the NSF program officer and project principal investigators (PIs) and evaluators felt this evaluation "didn't really tell the full story" of the impact of the CETP projects. As the NSF program officer stated, upon completion of the SRI evaluation, "We felt that there was a need to have [an evaluation] that worked with the projects, developed instruments where they needed to be developed, [so] that then everyone could contribute data to the core."

In 1999, building upon the recommendations from two meetings of the CETP project PIs, the NSF funded a new national, overarching program-level evaluation effort through a $990,000 grant to PI Frances Lawrenz at the University of Minnesota. The core evaluation used a mixed-methods design that included surveys of deans, faculty, principals, teachers, students, and NSF scholars; classroom activities assessments; and classroom observations. Core-evaluation personnel also convened meetings of grantees to develop standard data-collection instruments and to provide technical assistance on data collection and analysis.

NEW DIRECTIONS FOR EVALUATION • DOI: 10.1002/ev

In contrast to the summative evaluation conducted by SRI, the CETP core evaluation, as it was called, involved a significant number of CETP projects in the development and refinement of instruments and development of data-collection methods. Both NSF and Lawrenz had an implicit theory of action that guided the decision to involve projects in the evaluation design and instrumentation. The belief was that if projects were involved in the development of the evaluation, they would be more willing to participate in evaluation data-collection activities. Additionally, greater project involvement was believed to lead to the development of instruments that would be more contextually relevant to the local sites, therefore improving the validity of the collected data. Participation in all of the core-evaluation activities was voluntary on the part of the projects. In addition, the projects chose the extent of their involvement, both in the development of evaluation plans and instruments and in the collection and provision of evaluation data to the core evaluation for analysis.

Method

Data were collected through an on-line survey distributed to CETP project leaders and evaluators ($n = 54$), interviews with eight CETP project leaders (project primary investigators, coprimary investigators, coordinators, directors, administrators, or project consultants) or evaluators, and an interview with the NSF program officer responsible for the CETP program at the time. Additional data were collected through review of archival documents, publications, and reports produced by the CETP program and core evaluation and through reflections provided by the CETP core-evaluation PI.

Findings

Involvement

To the surprise of the core-evaluation team, the projects' requests for technical assistance and evaluation help, which resulted in the core evaluation being established, did not result in high levels of participation by all CETP projects. Data from the survey and interviews with CETP project PIs and evaluators found that levels and types of involvement in the CETP core evaluation varied across projects and individuals. Although the majority of respondents reported being involved, at least a little or some, in all of the aspects of evaluation planning, implementation, and communication, 22–48% responded that they were not involved in any individual activity.

As would be expected given the nature of the core evaluation, project PIs and evaluators reported being primarily involved in two stages: first, in the planning and instrument-development phase, and second, in the data-gathering phase. The interviews found that many project PIs and evaluators equated their involvement in the core evaluation with their participation in the evaluation instrument development activities. These activities took place

NEW DIRECTIONS FOR EVALUATION • DOI: 10.1002/ev

during a series of collaborative meetings facilitated by the core-evaluation team. As one project director shared, during the meetings "we really carved out the vision for what the core evaluation would be and what it would look like and what kind of data we might collect."

Providing data to the core-evaluation team was an additional way that many of the projects reported, through the survey and the interviews, that they were involved in the core evaluation. Some interviewees mentioned that they complied with core-evaluation requests for data and sent in data from their projects. One project PI stated, however, that the data-collection process was a large burden for her project. As she put it,

> We found that the expectation of sending out the student evaluation forms to teachers in classrooms, both those that had and had not been impacted by the original CETP project, and trying to get administrative responses and trying to get faculty responses was really a daunting task. And it used an immense amount of time . . .

Although the interview participants and survey respondents reported that they were involved with core data-collection activities, the data provided by the projects to the core evaluation were frequently incomplete. Although the core team welcomed participation by project PIs and evaluators in the development of the evaluation plans, they were surprised that this involvement did not lead to higher participation in data-collection activities. Despite the core's many incentives for participation, the substantial challenges of adding the core evaluation to their existing project evaluations rendered the incentives largely ineffective at obtaining participation by all the CETPs. In the end, only 12 of the 19 CETPs provided data to the core evaluation. Additionally, some CETPs submitted experimental data, whereas others submitted anecdotal data. Some CETPs trained observers and conducted classroom observations in one way, some in another. Not all projects submitted data from all of their participants; some projects collected data from only one subset of their project participants (for example, principals but not teachers, or teachers but not principals).

Use by Project PIs and Evaluators

Project PIs and evaluators reported on the survey that the CETP core evaluation had the greatest perceived effect on their knowledge and understandings, followed closely by effects on their skills and beliefs. Over 70% of all project leaders and evaluators who responded to the survey reported that the core evaluation increased their knowledge or understanding of evaluation stages; science, technology, engineering, and mathematics (STEM) education; STEM education evaluation; and their project, at least to a small extent. Approximately a quarter of respondents indicated that the evaluation influenced their knowledge and understandings extensively. Like the responses to questions about their knowledge and understandings, approximately 70% of respondents felt the core evaluation had at least a little influence on their evaluation and STEM education skills, although smaller percentages reported extensive influence in these areas (11–19%). The influence of the core evaluation on project leaders' and evaluators' beliefs was somewhat lower than the effect in the first two areas, with approximately one-third of all respondents indicating that there was no effect.

During the interviews, project leaders and evaluators provided more detailed information about the ways in which the evaluation increased their knowledge and skills. In terms of new knowledge, some interviewees mentioned that they learned about the importance of planning for evaluation early in a program's development. This occurred after they had seen the effects of implementing the core evaluation after many of the projects had already been funded for several years. CETP project leaders and evaluators also reported that they valued learning about issues facing their colleagues at other CETP projects around the country. Several reported feeling that they acquired a broader perspective about issues facing the STEM education field as a result of their attendance at the meetings. As one project PI reported,

> Anytime that Frances [core-evaluation PI] came to those meetings, it was very useful because she gave us that overview, that perspective of all the CETPs and what they were doing. Otherwise we were just isolated little people in our own institutions, with our own institutional problems . . . [I]t really broadened our viewpoints and perspectives.

In addition to a broader perspective, some interviewees also described that their participation in the evaluation led to building relationships with other CETP project leaders and evaluators across the nation. One project PI stated feeling that "the process of Frances doing the evaluation was useful to me because it gave me a perspective overall of the projects. And so I could see what other people did on their campuses and got to communicate with them." Similarly, another PI stated that she found the meeting she attended to be "useful in that it helped us a great deal in establishing relationships with other CETPs' project directors and learning the types of activities they were involved with, so they were helpful in terms of networking and collaboration."

Individuals who reported on the survey that they had been involved in an evaluation subsequent to their involvement in the CETP project were asked whether they had used the knowledge, products, or processes that arose from the core evaluation in another evaluation context. Over four-fifths of respondents indicated that they had used what they learned from planning and implementing the evaluation in another evaluation context. In fact, almost 60% of respondents indicated that they had used the program evaluation as a model for another evaluation, and two-thirds of respondents stated they had used data-collection instruments developed for the CETP core evaluation in another evaluation. This open-ended survey response illustrates this point. The respondent stated that "two doctoral students I have advised recently have selected the CETP adaptation of the Classroom Observation Protocol as one tool for data collection in their dissertation research."

Implications of Voluntary Project-Level Involvement

Although the NSF provided encouragement and the core evaluation provided incentives such as funding for data collection and data cleaning, participation in the core evaluation was completely voluntary for the CETP projects. The core team made considerable effort to include project representatives in developing evaluation plans and instruments to meet the projects' disparate needs. Lawrenz and the NSF program officer hoped that involvement in the development of evaluation instruments would increase the projects' commitment to providing data to the core and that the data would be seen as more valid.

Some of the project PIs and evaluators interviewed for this study felt that involvement in planning meetings did result in project leaders and evaluators feeling committed to the evaluation process and confident in the data-collection instruments. As one stated,

> . . . the way that [the core evaluation] was initially handled, how all the different projects were brought together, that there was a broad base of voices and perspectives in the initial planning group. I think those factors were both important to the success of the evaluation process as well as keeping the key players involved and committed to the process, and making sure that all kinds of projects were readily represented in the instruments that were created.

However, despite work to include all willing project PIs and evaluators in the development of instruments and evaluation plans, some individuals questioned the quality and value of common data collected from multiple sites. As one survey respondent wrote, the "CETP projects were quite diverse, and each had already designed its own evaluation. The overall, NSF evaluation compared apples and oranges (which negates validity), and in the process stifled the local evaluation efforts." Others stated that they felt the "quality" of the evaluation was compromised because it was designed in a collaborative fashion. Furthermore, others commented that the core evaluation did not fit their needs and, instead, was seen as an additional burden.

A positive outcome of involvement in planning the evaluation was that some project PIs and evaluators felt they learned a lot by participating in a collaborative process to try to evaluate the disparate projects. These individuals reported learning the complexities involved in that scale of evaluation and stated that they had applied their new understandings in future endeavors. Additionally, the collaborative process of development of the evaluation and instruments led to a feeling of community among some participating project PIs and evaluators.

In conclusion, the core evaluation created common instruments and provided technical assistance to the individual CETP evaluators to facilitate the evaluation of complex projects within the short evaluation period. Widespread participation in the early core meetings, however, did not translate into uniform collection of the data with the common instruments or uniform data sharing and reporting. In the end, the core-evaluation team sent evaluation reports to the NSF and to the CETP projects, but, with noncomparable data, was cautious in disseminating evaluation findings more broadly.

LIJA O. GREENSEID is a senior evaluator with Professional Data Analysts, Inc. in Minneapolis, Minnesota, and completed her Ph.D. in the Department of Educational Psychology at the University of Minnesota.

FRANCES LAWRENZ is the Wallace Professor of Teaching and Learning in the Department of Educational Psychology and the associate vice president for research at the University of Minnesota.

NEW DIRECTIONS FOR EVALUATION • DOI: 10.1002/ev

Roseland, D., Volkov, B. B., & Callow-Heusser, C. (2011). The effect of technical assistance on involvement and use: The case of a Research, Evaluation, and Technical Assistance project. In J. A. King & F. Lawrenz (Eds.), *Multisite evaluation practice: Lessons and reflections from four cases. New Directions for Evaluation, 129*, 33–38.

4

The Effect of Technical Assistance on Involvement and Use: The Case of a Research, Evaluation, and Technical Assistance Project

Denise Roseland, Boris B. Volkov,
Catherine Callow-Heusser

Abstract

In contrast to typical National Science Foundation program evaluations, the Utah State Math Science Partnership-Research, Evaluation and Technical Assistance Project (MSP-RETA) provided technical assistance (TA) in two forms: direct TA for up to 10 projects a year, and professional development sessions for a larger number of project staff. Not surprisingly, the two forms led to different results in terms of involvement and use. Most of those who participated in the direct technical assistance activities were positively affected and sought additional support and development. Project staff who were not included in the direct assistance efforts were more likely to report limited involvement and use. © Wiley Periodicals Inc., and the American Evaluation Association.

The National Science Foundation (NSF) Math Science Partnership (MSP) program began as a presidential initiative in 2001 and was authorized by Congress in 2002. MSP is a major research and development effort that supports innovative partnerships to improve K–12 math and science instruction, enhance student achievement, and reduce the achievement gap in math and science performance among diverse student populations. In that endeavor, MSP promotes efforts to develop partnerships between higher education and K–12 science, technology, engineering, and mathematics (STEM) teachers. The partnerships must support the program's goals to provide challenging coursework; increase the quantity, quality, and diversity of math and science teachers; and establish results-oriented projects that implement evidence-based educational practices. Typical project activities include new curriculum development and skill building for teachers. Successful projects serve as models that can be widely replicated. In 2006, MSP was bringing together 150 institutions of higher education, 550 school districts, and 3,300 schools, along with corporate partners, including Pfizer, Ford, Texas Instruments, Inc., Xerox, IBM, Merck, and Intel.

MSP–Research, Evaluation, and Technical Assistance Projects Overview and Activities

The MSP created a subset of projects dedicated to research, evaluation, and technical assistance (aptly titled Research, Evaluation, and Technical Assistance projects or RETAs). The MSP-RETAs conduct and support evaluation and research to improve K–12 STEM education. The RETA projects directly support the work of the MSPs, especially by developing tools to assess teachers' growth in the knowledge of mathematics or the sciences needed for teaching, conducting longitudinal studies of teachers and their students, or engaging the national disciplinary and professional societies in MSP work. Of the more than 30 MSP-RETA projects, this case study considers just one: the Utah State University MSP-RETA project, titled "Building Evaluation Capacity of STEM Projects–MSP," established in October 2002. Unlike almost all other MSP-RETA projects, the Utah State MSP-RETA received a grant of $1.5 million over 3 years; most of these projects received only 1 year of funding. A no-cost NSF grant extension and an additional supplemental grant of approximately $300,000 helped continue the work of the Utah State MSP-RETA for a fourth year.

The purpose of the Utah State MSP-RETA was not to evaluate MSP projects per se, distinguishing it from many NSF evaluations. Rather, this RETA was funded to provide direct technical assistance to 10 MSP projects per year related to identifying evaluation needs, developing program evaluation models based on those needs, and building evaluation capacity within those projects. Further, this RETA offered technical assistance and expert consultation via a network of evaluation consultants and supported the development of professional communities of teachers, researchers, evaluators, cognitive scientists, and social scientists, as well as others who depended on evaluation for continued improvement and generating new knowledge. To that end, the Utah State MSP-RETA created program-wide evaluation assistance in the form of educational seminars, conferences, materials, and individualized technical assistance both for projects receiving direct technical assistance and other MSPs from across the country, as space allowed. Through these activities with local MSP projects, the Utah State MSP-RETA informed and promoted evaluation at the project level, but did not engage in core MSP evaluation activities or conduct evaluations of local projects.

Given the project-driven nature of the Utah State MSP-RETA, evaluation questions and designs were determined in collaboration with project staff to meet local contextual needs of the projects receiving direct assistance. The Utah State MSP-RETA project also worked to develop state-of-the-art evaluation models for STEM education projects. For example, the Utah State RETA developed and disseminated the Design–Implementation–Outcomes (DIO) cycle that incorporated elements of evidence-based evaluation design, per the request of NSF's MSP (Callow-Heusser, Torres, & Chapman, 2005). The DIO cycle provided a framework for considering project activities at multiple levels and from multiple perspectives. The Utah State RETA staff intended that evaluations designed with input from the DIO cycle would provide evidence for accountability, improve projects, and support the value and feasibility of projects and activities. In addition to the DIO cycle, the Utah State RETA developed an on-line logic-model tutorial and a database of on-line evaluation resources for use by local project staff.

Method

This chapter presents empirical data to describe what involvement in the Utah State MSP-RETA technical assistance activities meant to the projects. In addition, it presents empirical data on the subsequent use of the evaluation process and findings on the projects. Data for this research were collected through interviews with eight MSP project leaders and evaluators and an interview with the NSF program officer responsible for the MSP program at the time. Additional data were collected through review of archival documents, publications, and reports produced by the MSP Program and the Utah State MSP-RETA Project and through the Utah State MSP-RETA principal investigator's (PI's) reflections.

Findings

Involvement

The interview data suggested low to moderate feelings of involvement by MSP-RETA participants. When asked about the ways in which they were involved in the Utah State MSP-RETA evaluation-related activities (if any), interviewees identified two forms of involvement: needs assessment facilitated by the Utah State MSP-RETA, and community building in the form of networking and opportunities to share. Because the role of the Utah State MSP-RETA was to provide technical assistance rather than to evaluate projects, several respondents noted that the direct technical assistance process

NEW DIRECTIONS FOR EVALUATION • DOI: 10.1002/ev

with the Utah State MSP-RETA allowed them to make requests for specific or tailored support, and this was interpreted as a vehicle for involvement as well.

Use by Project PIs and Evaluators

In general, results from the interviews suggested that participation in the Utah State MSP-RETA evaluation-capacity building activities did prompt evaluation use by project leaders and evaluators, and in some cases extensively. Four of eight interviewees believed that evaluation model development was useful as a result of their involvement in the Utah State MSP-RETA activities. Interviewees provided the following examples of use:

Learned more about STEM
Became motivated to write and disseminate
Increased their network of professional colleagues across the country
Reworked the project model after participation in one of the professional development opportunities offered by the Utah State MSP-RETA

However, several interviewees noted that the Utah State MSP-RETA framework was not applicable to their MSP project and therefore did not promote use within their projects.

Interviewees were asked to identify reasons that the Utah State MSP-RETA affected their projects. Six of eight interviewees reported that they strengthened and deepened their knowledge base on evaluation as a result of their involvement in Utah State MSP-RETA activities. In addition, interviewees provided more examples of the Utah State MSP-RETA on their project:

Gaining feedback on evaluation plans
New knowledge and skills in evaluation planning and tasks
Motivation to share evaluation results with the field and other partners

Factors Related to the Extent and Type of Effects

Interviewees also reported that the major factors that enabled the Utah State MSP-RETA to affect them and their projects were as follows:

Responsiveness and expertise of the Utah State MSP-RETA leadership
Knowledgeable, helpful, and caring people with the Utah State MSP-RETA
Utah State MSP-RETA staff availability, flexibility, and timeliness of individual support and technical assistance, as well as group professional development opportunities
Professionalism and level of expertise that were present at professional development activities

However, interviewees also identified a number of factors that limited the influence of the Utah State MSP-RETA within their projects. Some reported that competing priorities like distance, travel time, and ability to travel to meetings with Utah State MSP-RETA staff limited the influence MSP-RETA activities had on them personally or on their projects. In addition, interviewees noted the Utah State MSP-RETA offered only limited time and resources to their local program. For example, one respondent explained that there was a limit based on RETA project funds to the amount of time and intellectual investment they could get from their MSP-RETA staff consultant. Another noted there simply was not enough MSP-RETA staff available at certain times because of the overlapping timelines of the MSP projects served. Still another wished that more funds had been available to involve more local project staff in the MSP-RETA professional development opportunities. In addition, several interviewees noted that the Utah State MSP-RETA framework was not applicable for their MSP project and therefore did not allow for much program or personal use to occur.

Implications

Several themes arose in the interviews related to project involvement in the Utah State MSP-RETA activities and ultimately the use of learning that resulted from such involvement. For instance, limited involvement brought about by the fiscal restraints on the number of project staff who could attend MSP-RETA activities ultimately translated into limited use for several of the projects involved. In addition, the timing of involvement may also have limited evaluation use in some projects. Likewise, these same restraints may have made it difficult for the Utah State MSP-RETA to ascertain the needs of and provide proper assistance to the projects involved. This might explain why some participants felt the Utah State MSP-RETA design was not appropriate for their project.

Ultimately, the interviews showed that use was affected by two distinctly different levels of involvement: the 10 MSP projects annually that were involved in the funded direct technical assistance activities provided by the Utah State MSP-RETA, and the other MSP projects at large who took part in the more broad conference and resource-sharing activities offered. Most of those who participated in the direct technical assistance activities were positively affected and wanted even more support and development. Projects not included in the funded direct assistance efforts of the Utah State MSP-RETA were more likely to report limited influence. These projects attended conferences hosted by the Utah State MSP-RETA and participated in other resource-sharing efforts. However, they did not receive the same level of fiscal support to attend the conferences and received no direct consultative support from the MSP-RETA staff. Perhaps the lesson learned from these examples is that these findings are related to the alignment of good intentions and project financial resources; the idea that often, unless we are required to do something and money is allocated to support the activity, there is not the motivation, the time, or the money to do it. Ultimately, financial resources of the Utah State MSP-RETA limited the number of projects who received direct TA. Although other projects may have wanted to or even needed to participate, they were not able to find the time or were prevented from participating because of resource limitations.

Of particular note is the high level of participation in the Utah State MSP-RETA conferences. The conferences were reportedly well-designed and accessible to project staff; they required less of a time and resource commitment than ongoing local evaluation knowledge and skill development, as well as capacity-building efforts. However, restrictions were placed on the number of project staff who could be involved because of funding limitations. After all, the Utah State MSP-RETA only had financial resources to support a limited number of people involved in a few projects, thus the influence of those efforts primarily affected those people. Perhaps this is an indication of the limited ways in which participants in professional development are able to return to their projects or organizations and share their newly gained knowledge and skills in such a way that it influences others in the project or organization.

Reference

Callow-Heusser, C., Torres, R. T., & Chapman, H. J. (2005). *Evidence: An essential tool. Planning for and gathering evidence using the design-implementation-outcomes (DIO) cycle of evidence.* Washington, DC: National Science Foundation. Retrieved from http://www.nsf.gov/pubs/2005/nsf0531/nsf0531.pdf

DENISE ROSELAND is a program evaluation consultant working with clients in public education and public health, and a doctoral candidate in the Department of Organizational Leadership, Policy, and Development at the University of Minnesota.

BORIS B. VOLKOV is an assistant professor of evaluation studies with the Center for Rural Health and Department of Family and Community Medicine at the University of North Dakota School of Medicine and Health Sciences. He completed his Ph.D. in Educational Policy and Administration at the University of Minnesota.

CATHERINE CALLOW-HEUSSER is president of EndVision Research and Evaluation, LLC, in Logan, Utah, and previously served as principal investigator on an NSF Mathematics–Science Partnership Research, Evaluation, and Technical Assistance Grant at Utah State University.

NEW DIRECTIONS FOR EVALUATION • DOI: 10.1002/ev

Roseland, D., Greenseid, L. O., Volkov, B. B., & Lawrenz, F. (2011). Documenting the impact of multisite evaluations on the science, technology, engineering, and mathematics field. In J. A. King & F. Lawrenz (Eds.), *Multisite evaluation practice: Lessons and reflections from four cases. New Directions for Evaluation, 129,* 39–48.

5

Documenting the Impact of Multisite Evaluations on the Science, Technology, Engineering, and Mathematics Field

Denise Roseland, Lija O. Greenseid, Boris B. Volkov, Frances Lawrenz

Abstract

This chapter discusses the impact that four multisite National Science Foundation (NSF) evaluations had on the broader field of science, technology, engineering, and mathematics education and evaluation. Three approaches were used to investigate the broader impact of these evaluations on the field: (a) a citation analysis, (b) an on-line survey, and (c) surveys and follow-up interviews with NSF project principal investigators (PIs). The results indicate that the four evaluations had at least some impact. In addition, they show that the four efforts had differential impact, generally related to the way each evaluation operated. Evaluations in operation for longer time periods produced more products with more types of dissemination. The most-cited products tended to be instruments and tools. The field influence survey showed that, overall, few NSF PIs had any knowledge of influential evaluations, evaluation publications, or evaluators. © Wiley Periodicals, Inc., and the American Evaluation Association.

T he case examples examined the effects that four National Science Foundation (NSF) program evaluations had on their respective project personnel. The purpose of this chapter is to discuss the impact that the four evaluations had on the broader fields of science, technology, engineering, and mathematics (STEM) education and evaluation. The broad impact or influence of evaluations is a relatively new topic in the evaluation community, as demonstrated in theoretical articles published by Kirkhart (2000), Mark and Henry (Henry & Mark, 2003; Mark & Henry, 2004), and Alkin and Taut (2003) and by empirical investigations conducted by Weiss and colleagues (Weiss, Murphy-Graham, & Birkeland, 2005), and by Christie (2007). The issue is of particular interest in large multisite evaluations because of the sizeable amount of public funds used to support both the projects and their related evaluation efforts. The notion of affecting the field is inherent in the dissemination requirements of most NSF grants and in the four highlighted evaluations. Specifically, although the evaluations were conducted to provide information to NSF staff, the NSF also encouraged the four evaluation principal investigators (PIs) to extend the impact of their work to the broader community through various types of dissemination.

Three approaches were used to investigate the broader impact of these four evaluations on the field: (a) a citation analysis, (b) an on-line survey, and (c) surveys and follow-up interviews with NSF project PIs. These approaches complemented each other by examining impact from different directions. First, the citation analysis measured the extent to which products (for example, evaluation reports, journal articles, conference presentations, and evaluation instruments) had been cited within articles and other works produced in the STEM evaluation and education fields. This analysis began by examining the products from the evaluation projects and then broadening its look out to the field. The on-line field-influence survey took a different tack and investigated which evaluations people in the field deemed to have been the most influential, thereby beginning with the field and looking back to the program evaluations. Finally, the surveys and follow-up interviews asked the participating project PIs, those members of the field most closely associated with the four evaluations, what they believed had been the broader impacts of their evaluation efforts on the field. The methods and findings from all of these studies are described briefly below.

Citation Analysis

For the citation analysis, impact was conceptualized as the use and influence of knowledge products that the program evaluations generated and disseminated.

Citation is a direct measure of influence on the literature of a subject, and it is also a strong indicator of scientific contribution, because it is derived from patterns of interaction among millions of published articles. When one researcher cites another's work, he/she is acknowledging the relevance of that work to the current study (ISI/Thomson Scientific, 2007)

Web of Science, Google Scholar, and Google were used to collect citation information from lists of evaluation products produced by the four evaluations. The lists of program evaluation products were compiled for each program evaluation by reviewing the PI's curriculum vitae and program evaluation archives and through Internet Web searches. A variety of search terms were used, and inter- and intrarater reliabilities were checked to guarantee that the citations identified were accurate and as complete as possible. Despite careful cross checking there are always limitations in any searching process, such as time boundedness; therefore the citations that were found in this study should be seen as only a cross-sectional sample of the true citations to the works. (Discussion of differences in the results obtained through the three search engines, as well as other technical and validity aspects of citation analysis, is explored in more detail in Greenseid, 2008.)

Among the four evaluations, a total of 246 evaluation products were produced through the end of 2006, including one product that was informed by three of the four evaluations (Advanced Technological Education [ATE], Collaboratives for Excellence in Teacher Preparation [CETP], and Local Systemic Change for Teacher Enhancement [LSC]). Each evaluation produced different quantities and/or types of products. Types of evaluation products included instruments/tools, presentations, publications, dissertations, newsletters, and reports. Coincidentally, both ATE and LSC produced a total of 98 products each, and CETP and the Math Science Partnership–Research, Evaluation and Technical Assistance Project (MSP-RETA) produced 24 and 25 products, respectively. It is not surprising that the ATE and LSC evaluations produced the most products, as they were funded at higher levels and for longer time frames. Also, in their last years of funding, both the ATE and LSC evaluations emphasized dissemination of findings to the field.

A total of 377 references to the 246 evaluation products were found. The 377 references were found in 280 unique articles. Although the vast majority of the articles only cited one product ($n = 223$), 39 of the articles cited two evaluation products, 11 cited three products, and the remaining 7 cited more than three products. One article cited 14 of the products examined in this study. This was the capstone report produced by the LSC core-evaluation team (Banilower, Smith, Weiss, & Pasley, 2006). The mean number of citations per product for each of the evaluations ranged from 0.4 for the MSP-RETA to 2.53 for LSC with ATE at 0.65 and CETP at 1.75. Interestingly, however, post hoc analyses of differences between the evaluations showed that the only significant difference in mean product citation counts was between the ATE evaluation and the LSC core evaluation.

Evaluation reports accounted for almost 50% of the products that the four program evaluations produced in aggregate; however, within each evaluation the distribution varied. Over half of the products ATE produced were evaluation reports ($n = 52$), whereas presentations ($n = 27$) and publications ($n = 19$) comprised the remaining half. ATE did not publish any evaluation instruments or tools. CETP produced almost equal numbers of instruments ($n = 5$), reports ($n = 5$), and publications ($n = 4$), and a number of presentations as well ($n = 10$). LSC produced 42 evaluation reports and 33 publications. The remaining products produced by LSC were instruments ($n = 13$) and presentations ($n = 10$). MSP-RETA focused on presentations ($n = 18$). The remaining quarter of MSP-RETA products were reports ($n = 4$), instruments ($n = 2$), and publications ($n = 1$). The one multievaluation product was a publication in the *American Journal of Evaluation*. Evaluation instruments and tools were cited most frequently, averaging 7.25 citations per product. This was significantly higher than the other three product types, which ranged between 0 citations per presentation to 1.72 citations per report.

To get a more specific picture of products that were particularly influential in terms of being highly cited, the top 5% ($n = 13$) of cited products were analyzed in more depth. These highly cited works received a total of 230 of the 377 total references found in this study. In other words, the top 5% of evaluation products accounted for 61% of the total citations received by all 246 products. The majority of these works were evaluation instruments, such as classroom observation or professional development protocols, survey questionnaires, and data-collection manuals. Many of the others were products that presented descriptions of evaluation models or methods. The remaining highly cited products were interim or capstone reports from the LSC evaluation, and one was a technical report regarding surveys used in the LSC core evaluation. Citations to the highly cited products were split between external sources and those connected to one of the program evaluations. Approximately 55% of the citations to the highly cited works came from sources not affiliated with the four program evaluations and their staffs, and the other 45% were from sources connected to the four program evaluations.

Field-Influence Survey

As mentioned above, the field influence survey complemented the citation analysis in that it started with the field and then focused in to determine if the reported impact could be related to any of the four program evaluations. PIs of active NSF grants in the Directorate for Education and Human Resources (EHR) were selected as an appropriate, representative sample of the STEM education field. At the time of the survey there were a total of 2,301 eligible awards. The PIs represented various NSF organizations and programs, as well as universities and research institutions from the 50 United States. From that data set, SPSS software was used to draw a random sample of 350 individuals to complete the field-influence survey.

The survey was subjected to rigorous development procedures including team critique, think alouds, and two rounds of pilot testing. The final version of the survey was composed of 12 multiple-choice and 8 open-ended items. The first three questions asked the PIs if they were familiar with one or more influential, large scale, multisite STEM education evaluations; one or more influential publications prepared/disseminated by large-scale, multisite STEM education evaluations; and one or more influential evaluators who have conducted large-scale, multisite STEM education evaluations. Based on their responses, the survey takers were automatically triaged to the follow-up questions eliciting responses about PIs' perceptions of which specific evaluations, publications, and evaluators might have influenced the field of STEM education. Respondents were also asked why the listed material was influential. All were also asked demographic questions and if they had any involvement in the four evaluations. The overall response rate was 54.7%.

Slightly fewer than half (42.4%) of all respondents were able to provide an evaluation, publication, or evaluator by name. Of those who could provide an answer, most respondents were able to list an item in each category of evaluation, publication, and evaluator. It was rare that a respondent would list something in only one of the three categories. The reasons respondents cited for an evaluation's, a publication's, and an evaluator's influence differed. For instance, when citing the top reasons an evaluation was influential, respondents were most likely to say because it was an evaluation of an important program. In contrast, the top reason for a publication being considered influential was that it contained qualitative and quantitative findings. Finally, the top reason given for an evaluator being considered influential was his or her knowledge of STEM.

Not surprisingly, a majority of the respondents mentioned evaluation reports and other publications from evaluations associated with NSF programs:

Named evaluations associated with NSF programs   62.5%
Named publications associated with NSF programs   56.1%

Although, as shown above, most of the named evaluations were associated with NSF, there was diversity in the actual type of program to which the named evaluations were related, as shown in Table 5.1.

Similarly, examination of the NSF program associated with the named publication showed that most of the publications named were associated with NSF programs other than the four being studied in this project. Table 5.2 shows the type of program to which the named publications were related.

To investigate the impact of the four evaluation efforts on the field, the responses to the field-influence survey were examined in light of their relationships to the four efforts. Within the group of 64 respondents who could name an evaluation, 15 (38%) named an evaluation associated with ATE, CETP, LSC, or MSP-RETA. Within the group that could name an evaluation publication, 29.6% named an evaluation associated with ATE, CETP, LSC, or MSP-RETA; 9.1% identified publications associated with each (ATE, $n = 4$; LSC, $n = 4$; and MSP-RETA, $n = 4$; and 2.3% identified a publication associated with CETP, $n = 1$). When evaluations and publications named were combined, MSP-RETA evaluations and publications were noted by 10 respondents, ATE and LSC were each noted by 8 respondents, and CETP

Table 5.1. Named Evaluation by Program Association

Named Evaluation by Program Association		n
Associated with ATE, CETP, LSC, or MSP-RETA	37.5%	15
Associated with other NSF programs	52.1%	25
Associated with other federal non-NSF programs	10.4%	5
Associated with local or privately funded programs	6.3%	3

Table 5.2. Named Publication by Program Association

Named Publication by Program Association		n
Associated with ATE, CETP, LSC, or MSP-RETA	29.6%	13
Associated with other NSF programs	43.2%	19
Associated with other federal non-NSF programs	11.4%	5
Associated with local or privately funded programs	15.9%	7

was noted twice. Of the few respondents who could name an evaluator, most named unique individuals. Four evaluators were named by two respondents each, one evaluator was named by three respondents, and one was named by seven. The two evaluators named the most were from one of the four evaluation efforts.

All field-influence survey respondents were asked if they had been involved in any way with the four projects. The number of respondents reporting being involved ranged from 21 for ATE to 8 for MSP-RETA to 4 for CETP and 2 for LSC. Only a subset of those reporting being involved in ATE, MSP-RETA, CETP, or LSC, however, named an evaluation, an evaluation publication, or an evaluator. Of the 21 respondents who reported being involved in ATE, four identified evaluation reports as the most influential type of publication for their work. In addition, three of these same respondents identified an ATE-affiliated evaluation, publication, or evaluator by name. Two others identified other NSF evaluations, publications, or evaluators as influential to their work. Of the eight reporting involvement in MSP-RETA, three identified something from the MSP-RETA as influential. Of the four CETP-involved respondents, only two reported an evaluation, an evaluation publication, or an evaluator, and only one was related to the CETP evaluation effort. Both of the respondents reporting involvement in LSC named an evaluation, publication, or evaluator, but only one of the two was related to the LSC evaluation effort.

Surveys and Follow-Up Interviews With Project PIs

As described in the cases in Chapters 2–5, individual telephone interviews were conducted with project leaders from each of the four projects being investigated in order to understand the influence of the evaluation efforts on the individual projects. During these interviews, interviewees were also asked what impact the evaluation efforts had on the STEM education and evaluation fields. The results from these interviews are provided below.

Effects on the STEM Field

When asked about the ways in which the evaluation efforts had an effect on the STEM education field, interview participants noted that the most important lasting effect of the evaluations was a better understanding of evaluation, which can contribute to "the quality of evaluation in general and the public's perception and understanding of what is working." Providing diverse opportunities for individuals in the field of STEM education to improve skills was also described as important. One project leader reported that the STEM education field specifically may benefit from an evaluation because it creates methods for documenting and disseminating project activities. Consider the following quotation:

> . . .[W]hat we don't do a very good job with is documenting what the impact and outcomes of those activities are, and I think the Western Michigan project is very similar to addressing student outcomes at a university or community college. We know that we're teaching students, and we know that they're very successful at becoming employed and completing the programs, but we don't do a good job of documenting that. I think what the Western Michigan project does for NSF/ATE is it provides an actual format for documenting what those outcomes and impact have not only on our local community, but also on a national basis . . . Again, I think it helps not only collect that information, but also disseminate that so then you can go to the brochures, with the literature on the website and identify what . . . again, to see what actual impact that had, in terms of STEM projects in education.

Likewise, one interviewee associated with a peer-reviewed journal in the field offered evidence of this influence as follows:

> I see a lot of manuscripts that come through [where] the LSC classroom observation protocol has been used in so many grants and so many other programs nationwide that I think it really was never intended to be that way. . . . [T]hey were intended for the LSC, but subsequently so many other programs around the country have used that observation protocol.

One respondent, however, felt strongly that the core evaluation was instrumental in improving the culture of STEM teaching because it brought educators together to talk about common issues as part of the evaluation planning and training activities. As the interviewee explained,

> Everybody was teaching in inefficient ways, and [they] weren't concerned about teacher preparation as we all should be. And yet there was a core group of faculty in each university who each championed the cause. And I think that, more than anything, a result of the NSF project was that over the whole country there was a change in the culture of teaching. We can see it today. It was very influential.

Effects on the Evaluation Field

Interviewees were less likely to cite distinct ways in which the evaluation field had been influenced by any of these evaluations. However, one PI speculated that the ATE evaluation effort could have an impact if evaluators were "looking for guidelines and examples of a good evaluation project that will be very helpful for them." People did note that the evaluation field may be influenced through the evaluation capacity building activities in some of the evaluation efforts, as shown in the following example:

> I think of myself as an example of someone who prior to interacting with the RETA did not know much about program evaluation. I would have learned something about it simply by working in MSP, but when we think about larger capacity building or building the knowledge of individuals who are doing evaluation, I think that that's one impact both within and then beyond the MSP community. . .

Discussion

The results of these three examinations of impact on the field indicate that the four evaluation efforts had at least some impact. It must be kept in mind, however, that all three research methods had limitations, and all were likely to underestimate the actual effect of the evaluation efforts on the fields of STEM education and evaluation. The results show that the four efforts had differential impact, generally related to the way each evaluation operated.

The citation analyses suggest that evaluation efforts in operation for longer time periods produce more products with more types of dissemination. In addition, the most cited products tended to be instruments and tools. In contrast, the program evaluations that concentrated more on presentations, for example, MSP-RETA, were less likely to be cited than efforts that focused on publications.

The field influence survey showed that, overall, few of the NSF PIs surveyed had any knowledge of influential evaluations, evaluation publications, or evaluators. When they did have knowledge, it was most likely related to NSF programs. However, this link to NSF was not the primary reason for the influence, given that there was also diversity in the reasons why evaluations, evaluation publications, and evaluators were perceived to be influential. Although the data were limited by the small number of respondents, it did appear that more of the references than might be expected were associated with the four evaluations. There appeared to be little relationship between involvement in the ATE, CETP, LSC, or MSP-RETA evaluation efforts and consideration of the respective program evaluation effort as influential, but the numbers were very small. Despite the limited sample, the fact that respondents did mention evaluations, publications, and/or evaluators associated with the evaluation efforts suggests that these four efforts did have at least some impact on the field of NSF FHR PIs.

The survey and follow-up interviews with project PIs showed that project leaders and evaluators found it difficult to speak to the impact on the evaluation and STEM education communities, as they felt that they did not have broad enough understandings of the fields to comment accurately. Additionally, as one interviewee explained, it is hard to pinpoint changes in the field specifically to the activities of these evaluation efforts. Still, examples were seen that noted how positive it was to encourage people to do better evaluation, build their skills in conducting sound evaluations, and help them evaluate their initiatives in such a way that the results would inform practice in STEM. In addition, some perceived the expectation that evaluation findings would be disseminated to be a positive influence in their own project evaluations.

References

Alkin, M., & Taut, S. (2003). Unbundling evaluation use. *Studies in Educational Evaluation, 29*(1), 1–12.

Banilower, E. R., Smith, S. P., Weiss, I. R., & Pasley, J. D. (2006). The status of science teaching in the United States. In D. W. Sunal & E. Wright (Eds.), *The impact of state and national standards on K–12 science teaching* (pp. 83–122). Charlotte, NC: Information Age Publishing.

Christie, C. (2007). Reported influence of evaluation data on decision makers' actions: An empirical examination. *American Journal of Evaluation, 28*(1), 8–25.

Greenseid, L. O. (2008). *Using citation analysis methods to assess the influence of stem education evaluation* (Unpublished doctoral dissertation). University of Minnesota, Minneapolis.

Henry, G. T., & Mark, M. M. (2003). Beyond use: Understanding evaluation's influence on attitudes and actions. *American Journal of Evaluation, 24*(3), 293–314.

ISI/Thomson Scientific. (2007). *How do we identify highly cited researchers?* Retrieved from http://isihighlycited.com.floyd.lib.umn.edu/isi_copy/howweidentify.htm

Kirkhart, K. E. (2000). Reconceptualizing evaluation use: An integrated theory of influence. *New Directions for Evaluation, 88,* 5–23.

Mark, M. M., & Henry, G. T. (2004). The mechanisms and outcomes of evaluation influence. *Evaluation, 10,* 35–56.

Weiss, C. H., Murphy-Graham, E., & Birkeland, S. (2005). An alternate route to policy influence: How evaluations affect D.A.R.E. *American Journal of Evaluation, 26*(1), 12–30.

DENISE ROSELAND *is a program evaluation consultant working with clients in public education and public health, and a doctoral candidate in the Department of Organizational Leadership, Policy, and Development at the University of Minnesota.*

LIJA O. GREENSEID *is a senior evaluator with Professional Data Analysts, Inc., in Minneapolis, Minnesota. She earned her Ph.D. in the Department of Educational Psychology at the University of Minnesota.*

BORIS B. VOLKOV *is an assistant professor of evaluation studies with the Center for Rural Health and Department of Family and Community Medicine at the University of North Dakota School of Medicine and Health Sciences. He completed his Ph.D. in Educational Policy and Administration at the University of Minnesota.*

FRANCES LAWRENZ *is the Wallace Professor of Teaching and Learning in the Department of Educational Psychology and the associate vice president for research at the University of Minnesota.*

NEW DIRECTIONS FOR EVALUATION • DOI: 10.1002/ev

Lawrenz, F., King, J. A., & Ooms, A. (2011). The role of involvement and use in multisite
evaluations. In J. A. King & F. Lawrenz (Eds.), *Multisite evaluation practice: Lessons and
reflections from four cases. New Directions for Evaluation, 129,* 49–57.

6

The Role of Involvement and Use in Multisite Evaluations

Frances Lawrenz, Jean A. King, Ann Ooms

Abstract

*A cross-case analysis of four National Science Foundation (NSF) case studies
identified both unique details and common themes related to promoting the use
and influence of multisite evaluations. The analysis provided evidence of diverse
evaluation use by stakeholders and suggested that people taking part in the multisite evaluations perceived their involvement differently from the more traditional view of participation in local evaluations. The study also highlighted the
importance of attending to the following issues: the interface between the funder and local project staff; the life cycles of the program and its evaluation, as
well as those of the local project and its individual staff; the details of who controls the projects; the many tensions that can exist between the goals of the large-
scale program and its smaller funded projects; the perceived quality of the
evaluation and the evaluators; and the possibilities of community building and
networking across projects.* © Wiley Periodicals Inc., and the American Evaluation Association.

The research that is the basis of this discussion focused on the evaluations of the four National Science Foundation (NSF) programs
described in brief case chapters: the Advanced Technology Education
Program evaluation, the Collaboratives for Excellence in Teacher Preparation

NEW DIRECTIONS FOR EVALUATION, no. 129, Spring 2011 © Wiley Periodicals, Inc., and the American Evaluation
Association.   Published online in Wiley Online Library (wileyonlinelibrary.com) • DOI: 10.1002/ev.354

Program evaluation, the Local Systemic Change Program evaluation, and the Utah State evaluation capacity building project for the Mathematics and Science Partnerships Program (MSP). The purpose of this cross-case analysis is to highlight similarities and differences across these cases to shed light on the role of involvement and use in large, multisite evaluations. The primary issue examined is the relationship between involvement in evaluation and the use of the evaluation by people other than the primary intended users (in this case, the NSF staff) and the practices that are most directly related to enhancing the evaluations' influence. The full case studies provide far more detail of the patterns of involvement and use that were part of these evaluations, and this analysis relies on the additional content of those longer versions.

These case studies operated in a unique space, crossing boundaries that have constrained previous evaluation research. First, although much of the research in evaluation has examined the effects of participation in evaluation on the use of evaluation processes and findings, these cases were not about participatory evaluation as commonly understood in the evaluation field (that is, an evaluation in a single place or with a finite group of people). Instead, this research addressed large multisite evaluations where the "participants" were defined not as individual people, but rather as individual projects, each implementing a different approach to solving a national problem at different sites across the country. Therefore, the study collected data from individual people serving as representatives of their projects. To highlight this distinction, we used the term *involvement* rather than *participation* (Lawrenz & Huffman, 2003; Toal, 2009; Toal, King, Johnson, & Lawrenz, 2009). Second, this research focused on the use of evaluation by secondary, somewhat unintended users. Although NSF was the primary user and client in each of the four program evaluation projects, the research team did not examine NSF's use of the evaluation process or findings, but rather focused on the local projects and on the fields of science, technology, engineering, and mathematics (STEM) education and evaluation, regardless of whether the national program evaluators were instructed to consider project and field use in the program evaluation design. Finally, the cases were all funded by the NSF and, necessarily, functioned within that context.

To understand the analysis, readers should keep the study's limitations in mind. It represents only four instances of large, multisite NSF evaluations, and therefore, although potentialities can be suggested, generalizations to other settings are not appropriate. The case studies themselves are based on self-report data, along with the analysis of archival records. The numbers of people surveyed and interviewed are small, but appear to be at least representative of the groups included. The instruments used for data gathering were developed as part of the project and therefore might not be ideally valid. Nevertheless, the ideas generated from the case studies provide direction for both research and practice, as shall be discussed.

NEW DIRECTIONS FOR EVALUATION • DOI: 10.1002/ev

Results

In the final analysis, the relationships between involvement and use remained unique in each case. Consider the following examples from each of the program evaluations that point to the variety of possibilities.

- In ATE, despite extensive dissemination efforts on the part of the evaluation project, local project staff did not report using or being influenced very much by the overall program evaluation data. Instead, the project participants often reported feeling involved through the act of completing the survey.
- In LSC, the extensive involvement of the projects, the required discussions between the local project evaluators and principal investigators (PIs), and the monitoring of the evaluation data that the projects provided to the core-evaluation team appeared to increase both the conceptual and the instrumental use of the evaluation results by project staff and people in the field. This arguably mandatory use was associated with greater project-level engagement with data-collection instruments, protocols, and data, and with greater interest in the overall results using both their and others' data. It also appears that there was more use of the eventual evaluation publications.
- In CETP, involvement reportedly produced positive feelings and a community of evaluators for those who chose to get involved. This involvement resulted in conceptual use in terms of knowledge, beliefs, and skills, but it did not appear to be related to instrumental or broad field use of the evaluation products.
- In the MSP, the relationship was more complex because of the options for different levels of participation that resulted from the range of evaluation-related services available, from direct technical assistance from an evaluation consultant to attendance at evaluation capacity-building workshops. As could be expected, there appeared to be more instrumental and conceptual use when there was individualized evaluation work, although the workshops appeared to result in conceptual use, primarily influencing dispositions toward evaluation.

Despite these differences, however, similarities across the four cases pointed to a number of shared themes. The themes presented below relate to the involvement of the local projects in the program evaluation and the subsequent use of evaluation processes and outcomes both by the local projects and by individuals in the fields of evaluation and STEM education. Six overarching themes emerged from the analysis across cases. They concerned the following topics, each of which will be discussed in more detail below: the NSF interface, life cycles, project control, tensions, the perceived quality of the evaluation/evaluator, and community building.

New Directions for Evaluation • DOI: 10.1002/ev

- The type of interface with NSF affected people's involvement and use. How NSF project officers viewed the involvement or cooperation of individual projects with the larger program evaluations varied and thus created different levels of interface between the funded projects and NSF. NSF requirements for program-level data, the potential for helping to develop instruments, and expectations for dissemination or outreach gave a message to local project staff that their participation in the evaluation mattered. The relationship with NSF clearly affected both involvement and use. Projects could view the program evaluators' relationship with NSF as a conduit for them, whereby evaluators played the role of buffer between projects and NSF personnel. Not surprisingly, projects were also more willing to be involved with and make use of evaluation processes and outcomes when they believed NSF supported the evaluation effort. When NSF supported dissemination, more attention to involvement with the field made sense to projects. In addition, if the field believed that NSF valued the results of the evaluations, people were reportedly more likely to use them.
- The life cycles of programs, projects, and individuals also affected people's involvement and use. Each local project had a unique life cycle that varied according to the timing of the program evaluation in relation to the program, the local project, and the individual project evaluation. Local project politics could dramatically affect people's ability to connect with the larger evaluation. The intersecting life cycles of the program evaluation, the local projects, and even the personnel at the local projects dramatically affected involvement and use. For example, a project leader who was having personal issues might be unable to continue work on the program evaluation, or if the local project evaluation was almost finished before staff members were asked to provide data to the program evaluation, data collection that duplicated earlier efforts might prove frustrating. Projects were more easily involved in evaluation efforts in their early stages of development when other goals were not in conflict with the evaluation's goals or when resources were not entirely committed elsewhere. Such involvement could lead to more use. Likewise, the life cycle of the evaluations and individuals affected involvement and use by the field. Not surprisingly, people in the field were more likely to engage with and use evaluation outcomes at the end of a program evaluation when the data were more complete and the lessons learned could be stated definitively and with more surety.
- The effect of local project control on involvement in and use of evaluation is nuanced. The amount of control a local project had over its involvement in the program evaluation was understandably related to the relationship between involvement and use of the evaluation processes and outcomes. Requiring participation, of course, resulted in involvement, but this mandatory or enforced involvement reportedly did not necessarily result in more use. Some people expressed frustration at mandated activities that

were not in sync with their local evaluation efforts. If the choice was left up to local project staff, complete local control resulted in less involvement because staff members were typically too busy conducting their own project evaluations to be engaged with the program evaluation. However, if local staff chose to be involved, their use of the outcomes was reportedly more likely because the evaluation was tailored more directly to their project's needs. The approach that seemed to result in the most involvement and use was one that required participation, but that also allowed local project staff to gather and interpret their own data, coupled with the opportunity for feedback to the larger program evaluation.

- Tensions between local project goals and program evaluation goals affected involvement and perhaps use. There was evidence in all four settings of tension between different alternatives, a double-edged sword related to resources. Should local project evaluation resources support activities related to the project itself or to the larger program evaluation? In the LSC, for example, all projects, big or small, had the same core-evaluation costs. This was a significant burden for the smaller projects, creating tension between projects. The issue arose when smaller projects could not find money to support activities in light of the high evaluation costs. In the ATE and CETP evaluations there were external problems with funding that resulted in delayed or changed activities and created tension about what to do when funding was not available. These tensions negatively affected involvement and possibly use. From the projects' staff perspectives, the evaluations might not be well aligned with their goals; therefore they reported being reluctant to participate and were sometimes skeptical about the validity of the results. Another critical tension concerned the balance between understanding the need for the national evaluations, while wanting to prioritize the local project evaluations because they potentially had a more direct effect on the projects. In general there was little evidence that these tensions affected involvement and use by the field, although low opinions of project staff might in some way have discredited evaluation outcomes for others connected to the projects.
- People were more likely to use the results of evaluations that they perceived as high quality or as the work of a highly competent evaluator. Project staff tended to report more use of the evaluation processes and outcomes when they were involved with what they viewed as high-quality evaluation efforts. This theme suggested that regardless of the amount or type of involvement, project staff might use evaluations more if they viewed the evaluators as well qualified. Use by the field also seemed to be affected by the evaluation's reputed quality. This appears to be related to dissemination in terms of how the evaluation outcomes are packaged and the need for the evaluation results in the field. People reported being more likely to use findings that were relevant to important issues in the field.
- Development of a community appeared to foster both involvement in the evaluation project and use of evaluation. Involvement in at least three of

New Directions for Evaluation • DOI: 10.1002/ev

the four evaluations facilitated the development of communities of practice or networks, and this was related to an increased perception of use of the evaluation processes and products. This theme emerged because it was often cited that involvement in a community of practice or network created the sense that people were part of a larger group and shared in its benefits. The more community-building efforts were supported, the more involved the projects reportedly felt. People perceived ongoing communication of all sorts, including asynchronous electronic communication, as helpful, but, importantly, for community building to occur at least some of the efforts needed to be face-to-face and focused on the evaluation. Clear evidence of mutual respect was also needed. Program evaluators had to be credible to project staff because of their recognized expertise, but at the same time they had to engage people, not lecture them or merely demand things. Development of community might be peripherally related to involvement and use by the field as projects that were part of the community brought in other members from the field.

Practicing evaluators know that the common answer to any question related to evaluations is that it depends. After several years of extensive research, what remains clear is that the relationship between involvement in a multisite program-level evaluation and the eventual use of its results depends on a number of factors. The study suggested the importance of attending to the following issues: the interface between the funder and the local project staff, the life cycles of the program and its evaluation as well as those of the local project and its individual staff, the details of who controls the projects, the many tensions that can exist between the goals of the large-scale program and its smaller funded projects, the perceived quality of the evaluation and the evaluators, and the possibilities of community building and networking across projects.

Discussion

The findings presented are unique in that they essentially introduce the study of evaluation use and involvement by *unintended* users. As described, the NSF funded the four evaluation projects, and NSF staff were the "primary intended users" (Patton, 2008) in all cases. Despite this fact, individual project staff and the fields of STEM education and evaluation were also important potential users. Their use of the evaluation processes and outcomes could be considered a bonus and a glimpse down the imagined pathways to the broader types of societal use that Mark and Henry (2004) propose. This research study developed new methods to ascertain the effect of involvement in and use of evaluation on unintended users such as project staff (for example, surveys of involvement and use) and fields (network analysis of citations and surveys of PIs and editors) as opposed to the effects on individuals.

Involvement of the local projects in the evaluations appears to be only one aspect promoting use of the evaluation processes and outcomes by the local projects. It seems to be an enabler in some instances, but not necessarily a strong or consistent one. Naturally, project personnel would have to know something about an evaluation to make use of it, but the case data suggest that the connection between knowing it and using it appears to be less than direct. Involvement can provide information about evaluation processes and products, and face-to-face presentations and other forms of dissemination and outreach may be necessary components of involvement. Involving more than one individual from each project increases the likelihood that someone will remain engaged. The creation of community appears to be a stronger force than individual involvement, although involvement could support its development.

Involvement by the field in general (as opposed to an individual) was less extensive. In fact, most involvement by the field tended to be embedded in the evaluation project's outreach and dissemination efforts, although some involvement was through the projects. Use by the field appeared to be promoted by close relationships of the evaluation to NSF, by the evaluation project providing instruments that could be used in other settings, and by the evaluation providing easily used or referenced summary materials. Overall, it appears that these four evaluation projects had little impact on the fields of STEM education and evaluation. This may be due to limitations in our ability to measure the effects. It may also be because in both STEM education and evaluation, information from one study is not tightly built upon in future studies, as is the case in the bench sciences. Perhaps it is because these are complex settings, and there are too many variables to consider simultaneously, along with individual motivational and other interaction effects. Also evaluation results are more often provided to and likely to be used by the intended users (NSF staff in this case), rather than the unintended user (the fields in this case). The synthesis of findings from diverse research and targeted use studies may help, over time, to increase impact.

Regardless, the results of this cross-case analysis point to several ideas for facilitating involvement and subsequent use of evaluation processes and outcomes by unintended audiences in multisite evaluations. The most important aspect of facilitating involvement and use appears to be careful and continuous communication by the evaluators to the participating projects, as well as to the field through a variety of media. It is important to have a clear interface with the direct user of the evaluations because this relationship may affect how the individual projects and the field interact with the evaluation. Evaluators need to be cognizant of the life cycles of the individuals and the projects involved in the evaluation and plan purposefully for different types of involvement and use. Multisite evaluators should expect tensions between the overall evaluation and the local projects and their evaluation efforts. A seemingly fruitful way to use evaluation funds may be to develop a sense of community among the local projects through face-to-face meetings as well as through other types of contact. Developing a community of practice with mutual respect and true interest in each other's ideas as well as reasonable expectations for participation is important.

Across all of the cases, the perceptions of involvement by the individuals in the projects were not consistent. Perceptions of degree of involvement varied by type of activity engaged in and by the demand of the activity. Additionally, individuals had their own idiosyncratic, and not necessarily consistent, standards for what it meant to be involved a lot or a little. Various involvement schemas have been proposed in the evaluation literature. The four cases confirm some parts of those schemas and also provide additional aspects (Toal et al., 2009). In general the literature considers involvement at different points in the evolution of an evaluation and considers it to include aspects of control over the evaluation design, implementation, or interpretation/communication of results, for example, helping to design evaluation questions and helping to interpret data (Cousins, 2003). Our data show, however, that in multisite settings at least two other activities—providing data and attending meetings—were also viewed as involvement.

Future work should include additional research on the causal nature of involvement with evaluation use. The themes presented here provide fruitful areas for investigation. Many have called for more theoretical and aligned work in evaluation so that studies can build more effectively on each other (Cousins, Goh, Clark, & Lee, 2004; Henry & Mark, 2003). This cross-case analysis potentially provides a strong baseline for more positivistic research. It will be important to develop strong theories about the relationship between involvement and use that could form the basis for hypothesis formulation and subsequent research. It may also be possible to examine the issues raised here through more quantitative path analytic procedures.

In summary, it appears that perceptions of involvement in these four multisite evaluations are different from the perceptions considered in traditional participatory evaluations. This is partially true because of the different levels of participants in a multisite evaluation, but also because of the different nature of the type of evaluation being conducted. In a multisite evaluation, although the participant is really a site or project rather than an individual, it is, of course, individuals at the project level who respond (Lawrenz & Huffman, 2003). These project-level participants are generally members of the project leadership as opposed to participants in the project, which would be the case in more traditional participatory evaluations. Additionally, the projects and the field were not the directly intended users of the evaluations; NSF staff was.

Further, it is clear that individuals themselves have quite diverse opinions of what constitutes involvement. They perceive involvement from a different perspective than evaluation authors, such as Burke (1998). The participants studied here were differentially affected by the depth and breadth of involvement in evaluation activities, and neither breadth nor depth was consistently predictive of perceived levels of involvement. This lack of consistency in perceived involvement makes measuring involvement in multisite settings quite challenging. A similar case could be made for perceived use. This suggests that any investigation of the relationship between involvement and use will require in-depth measurement and is likely to be substantially affected by the nature of the evaluation and by the characteristics of the individuals involved.

References

Burke, B. (1998). Evaluating for a change: Reflections on participatory methodology. *New Directions for Evaluation, 80,* 43–56.

Cousins, J. B. (2003). Utilization effects of participatory evaluation. In T. Kellaghan & D. L. Stufflebeam (Eds.), *International handbook of educational evaluation* (pp. 245–268). Boston, MA: Kluwer Academic.

Cousins, J. B., Goh, S. C., Clark, S., & Lee, L. E. (2004). Integrating evaluative inquiry into the organizational culture: A review and synthesis of the knowledge base. *Canadian Journal of Program Evaluation, 19*(2), 99–141.

Henry, G. T., & Mark, M. M. (2003). Beyond use: Understanding evaluation's influence on attitudes and actions. *American Journal of Evaluation, 24*(3), 293–314.

Lawrenz, F., & Huffman, D. (2003). How can multi-site evaluations be participatory? *American Journal of Evaluation, 24*(4), 471–482.

Mark, M. M., & Henry, G. T. (2004). The mechanisms and outcomes of evaluation influence. *Evaluation, 10,* 35–56.

Patton, M. Q. (2008). *Utilization focused evaluation* (4th ed.). Thousand Oaks, CA: Sage.

Toal, S. (2009). The validation of the evaluation involvement scale for use in multi-site settings. *American Journal of Evaluation, 30*(3), 349–362.

Toal, S., King, J. A., Johnson, K., & Lawrenz, F. (2009). The unique character of involvement in multi-site evaluation settings. *Evaluation and Program Planning, 32*(2), 91–98.

FRANCES LAWRENZ is the Wallace Professor of Teaching and Learning in the Department of Educational Psychology and the associate vice president for research at the University of Minnesota.

JEAN A. KING is a professor and director of graduate studies in the Department of Organizational Leadership, Policy, and Development at the University of Minnesota.

ANN OOMS is a senior lecturer in the Faculty of Health and Social Care Sciences at Kingston University and St. George's, University of London, United Kingdom. She completed her Ph.D. in the Department of Educational Psychology at the University of Minnesota.

NEW DIRECTIONS FOR EVALUATION • DOI: 10.1002/ev

King, J. A., Ross, P. A., Callow-Heusser, C., Gullickson, A. R., Lawrenz, F., & Weiss, I. R. (2011). Reflecting on multisite evaluation practice. In J. A. King & F. Lawrenz (Eds.), *Multisite evaluation practice: Lessons and reflections from four cases. New Directions for Evaluation, 129,* 59–71.

7

Reflecting on Multisite Evaluation Practice

Jean A. King, Patricia A. Ross, Catherine Callow-Heusser, Arlen R. Gullickson, Frances Lawrenz, Iris R. Weiss

Abstract

The lead evaluators for four large-scale multisite National Science Foundation evaluations discuss their experiences across time and space to explicate what they have learned as six lessons that may be of use to other multisite practitioners. The lessons relate to the control of decisions, use of the evaluation process and outcomes, supporting project staff in their evaluation work, serving as a buffer between the funder and projects, taking purposeful leadership around cultural issues, and the importance of high-quality evaluation designs. © Wiley Periodicals Inc., and the American Evaluation Association.

Upon the recommendation of the National Science Foundation's (NSF's) "Beyond Evaluation Use" (see "Editors' Notes," this issue) project's Advisory Committee, four experienced evaluators gathered for a day in Chapel Hill, NC, to reflect aloud on their experiences conducting large-scale multisite evaluations and to capture what they had collectively learned to benefit others engaged in such efforts. What follows are portions of the day's transcript, edited thematically as a set of six lessons with identities masked. The lessons are stated, briefly described, and then explained through dialogue.

Note: In the chapter's transcript sections, the names of the evaluators are omitted, and the evaluators are instead identified by number. Jean King served as the facilitator.

NEW DIRECTIONS FOR EVALUATION, no. 129, Spring 2011 © Wiley Periodicals, Inc., and the American Evaluation Association. Published online in Wiley Online Library (wileyonlinelibrary.com) • DOI: 10.1002/ev.355

Lesson 1

An evaluator managing a multisite evaluation can involve people in some ways to increase ownership, but should never relinquish control of decisions.

These experienced evaluators discussed issues of involvement, knowing that the specific evaluations they reflected on had been chosen because the amounts of interaction expected of project principal investigators (PIs) and other staff differed. The evaluators used two common types of activities to involve project staff with the hope of increasing commitment to the evaluation: (a) participation in the design, and (b) helping to develop instruments. A frequent issue was how to identify people to take part in these interactions. One thing was clear: Regardless of the tasks in which project staff took part, the evaluators thought it important to maintain strict control over the final design and instrumentation.

> Evaluator 4: We had more involvement early because of wanting to stabilize the instruments, then reached a point where there was no sense in having continued involvement in the instrument design. But we did have involvement in some other ways. It was my strategy for getting buy-in.
>
> Evaluator 1: Just to clarify, there was more involvement in the training materials than in the actual evaluation.
>
> Evaluator 4: . . .which was not up for grabs.
>
> Evaluator 1: So there was continuing involvement, but it was for something other than designing the evaluations.
>
> Facilitator: . . and purposefully to get people to own the evaluation.
>
> Evaluator 4: That was my purpose. The stated purpose was to improve the quality of the interpretations.
>
> Facilitator: To get people involved in your evaluation, did you invite specific people to participate?
>
> Evaluator 1: Yes, we invited everybody. We had planning meetings as we designed the evaluation. Everybody was invited, they were expected to come, and we paid for them to come.
>
> Evaluator 4: We had some things that involved everybody as well, like the PI meetings. Overall though, we tended to be more democratic and let people pick themselves to be involved. We did not select participants who we thought would be essential, so I didn't necessarily get the most influential people.
>
> Evaluator 2: We actually selected people pretty carefully based on who was doing evaluation work and who NSF thought would give viable help and invited them to help us design instruments. We didn't want such a large

group. We thought it would be difficult to deal with, so we kept it down to what we could keep in a small room and talk comfortably.

Evaluator 4: Did the projects that were not involved feel less ownership?

Evaluator 2: Probably.

Evaluator 4: Did that have negative consequences down the road?

Evaluator 2: Well, it's hard to know. Some things happened because some of the people weren't as involved and they didn't understand things as fully. So they had less buy-in, and we lost them. On the other hand, we would have lost some things by having too many people involved.

Evaluator 4: It may be that the better ones would have understood what you were doing whether or not they had been involved, and the less good ones might not have understood even if they had been involved.

Evaluator 2: They would have confused the situation.

Evaluator 1: As our evaluation project neared the end, we noticed that the projects that actually asked us for help were those with competent internal or external evaluators who weren't afraid of asking questions and asking for help. The projects with less effective evaluators or those with less evaluation training or experience closed the doors on us. We also had those large working meetings where most projects sent people to attend. Again, some of the projects that sent key people, like PIs and evaluators, had a fairly competent understanding of evaluation and came to learn more.

Facilitator: Are there any program evaluation activities that project people should not be involved in?

Evaluator 1: Crafting the final recommendations. You can get input, but you are responsible for what you're putting out there under your name. You can give them drafts and you get feedback, so they'd be involved in writing the report, but the final edit is yours.

Evaluator 4: But how is that different from getting input from them on the instruments? The final instrument is still your decision.

Evaluator 1: Yes, I agree.

Evaluator 4: I would agree that they can give input, but I wouldn't take a majority vote to decide on the instrument, or the recommendation, or the report, or anything else.

Evaluator 1: Exactly. I think that's fair.

Evaluator 4: I can't think of anything where they wouldn't be involved. But there's not much I'd let them be in charge of.

Evaluator 1: Almost nothing—I agree with that.

NEW DIRECTIONS FOR EVALUATION • DOI: 10.1002/ev

Lesson 2

A multisite evaluator can use the evaluation as an intervention to improve individual projects.

These multisite evaluations might have seemed distant to the many projects that comprised the program. Nevertheless, the evaluators gave numerous examples of how participation in the overarching program evaluations affected the individual projects, thus documenting multisite process use.

> Evaluator 2: The longer I mess with this stuff, the more I'm convinced that rather than being a measure of change, evaluation is the causal agent of change.

> Evaluator 4: Yes, and it helps define what you mean by change so people know what to shoot for.

> Evaluator 1: It creates a common language.

> Evaluator 2: We see this in talking about sustainability. It's not just knowing what sustainability means and reaching the understanding that we have quite different perceptions about it, but even the simple interpretation of words. When people finally understand what you're talking about, they can sort through that minefield and begin to work together. I think evaluation does that in ways that nothing else does.

> Evaluator 4: It operationalizes things. For example, we don't create the instruments in order to improve the projects, but as a result of creating the instruments we, in fact, do improve the projects because it helps people focus on what does the program content mean. . .One of the best things we did was to pay some PIs to observe classrooms of teachers who had been in their professional development sessions, and then write cases for us. This was a sobering experience for them because they discovered that just because they taught it, doesn't mean the teachers learned it. Our PIs were going into classrooms and seeing a travesty. If I were doing this over, in at least a few cases, I'd have the PI and the evaluator do such observations.

> Evaluator 2: It changes the way the PIs understand what they're about, and that's the essence of evaluation. Having learned that lesson once, that's probably going to last them for a lifetime . . . We've embedded items in the survey that would cause the projects to engage in their evaluation differently. It was designed to help them think about evaluation issues.

> Evaluator 4: Ours was as well. These multisite evaluations helped increase the capacity of the evaluations and helped increase the quality of the project.

> Evaluator 1: I agree. We would have discussions that involved people at very different levels of capacity—there were some highly sophisticated evaluators and some teachers and graduate students with little or no evaluation experience. These discussions would be about design, and we'd consider issues such

as how one design was not the best, whether you could do it this way, why we needed to have matched classes, why just any class wouldn't work, and why we had to have teachers with at least the same amount of experience because we couldn't use experienced teachers as comparison teachers for the ones who were in their second year of teaching. For some of them, this was a new idea.

Evaluator 4: I would argue that even if you're an extremely savvy person, you learn a ton by hearing how other people react to these sorts of discussions.

Evaluator 1: I really do think these multisite program evaluations produce a lot of capacity building.

Evaluator 4: It's interesting. In the case where capacity building was an explicit goal, the projects were all doing different evaluations, and there was no opportunity for dialogue around a single instrument. There was no one instrument that everybody was going to use. Ironically, even though in my case evaluation capacity was an unintended positive consequence, we may have built more evaluation capacity because of the vehicle of common instruments. Ain't that a kick in the head?

Evaluator 3: One of the biggest things you learn in doing a multisite and seeing different perspectives is interpersonal skills. When you're doing anything multisite, you get a view of the big picture, and that big picture becomes important in the feedback you give to sites. They can see what they're doing every day, but being able to see that broader perspective adds more to the evaluation than probably anything.

Evaluator 1: Just to emphasize that a little more, being involved or seeing that national picture helps the local projects to better understand their goals. It helps them be more aligned with the national program.

Evaluator 3: Yes, and to see the value that you contribute to that big picture.

Evaluator 4: I was struck by the power of evaluation as a tool for developing common visions and common language. I'm more explicit now about using the crafting of the evaluation as an opportunity to make sure we all mean the same thing. It really didn't startle me that instruments play an important role in helping to focus on goals. As tools for capacity building, multisite evaluations give you so much of an opportunity to do that. We don't get that capacity when everybody's rolling their own. I think that these provide opportunities for community building, opportunities for vision setting, and opportunity for knowledge generation.

Lesson 3

When possible, multisite evaluators should provide support for project staff to complete evaluation tasks.

NEW DIRECTIONS FOR EVALUATION • DOI: 10.1002/ev

Multisite evaluators may face a daunting task when they need project staff to complete evaluation tasks. These people are likely to be busy working on their own project-related activities and may not see the personal value of the overall program evaluation. Even those who perceive the value may find it time consuming to take part. To help project staff complete tasks required by the overarching evaluation, the evaluators suggested using resources to provide support that may increase staff buy-in to the evaluation process. They identified a middle zone where support may be most useful: when project staff feel fairly competent, but not expert in evaluation, and are willing and able to learn from the experience. People who feel less competent may not understand the value of participating; true experts do not need to participate.

Evaluator 4: Advice to someone about designing and implementing a multisite evaluation would include how to give the projects support and tools that are helpful to them. For example, we collected questionnaire data. It was easy for us to feed the data tables back to the projects. The evaluators would have had to do this if we hadn't. Everybody loved that. Who wouldn't love that?

Evaluator 1: As a former local evaluator for this evaluation, I can tell you that those tables gave us significance levels. I thought it was terrific.

Evaluator 4: Basically, it was looking for opportunities to buy cooperation. So one piece of advice is to try and figure out what people need to do anyway and make it easier for them to do it.

Evaluator 3: We would call and talk to PIs and evaluators, and they would say, "We're too busy, we don't want to change anything we're doing, we don't have the time to even consider it." So it became an interesting situation.

Evaluator 1: When projects accepted our evaluation assistance, it was clearly burdensome for them to give up a day of their time to accept our help. They thought it was valuable, but still they weren't doing all these other things that they wanted to do. The help wasn't coming on their time frame. It's just like doing an external evaluation. You show up and everything else stops because, oh well, the external evaluator's here now.

Evaluator 3: We gave projects choices for assistance. Finding matches that would work when projects requested assistance was a challenge.

Evaluator 1: We found that assistance didn't work so well for them because they felt they still had to do all this work themselves. What they wanted was somebody to come in and actually do the work. They didn't want advice.

Evaluator 4: I think what's going on here is sort of a capacity curve. If these people had all the capacity they needed and you weren't going to be useful, they weren't going to request assistance. If they had too little capacity to use the advice when advice was what you were giving, then the assistance wasn't enough to make a difference. There was a middle zone of people who had enough capacity to take advantage of the advice you were offering.

Evaluator 3: A narrow zone—a very narrow zone.

Evaluator 4: Assisting people in the middle zone made a big difference because they could learn about instruments or analyses they didn't know about or even a way to frame the evaluation that they wouldn't have thought about. In my evaluation there were some people for whom it saved time. There was nothing we did that they couldn't have done. There were other people for whom our instruments or our sampling enabled them to do things better than they otherwise would have. But then there were people who were forced to do what they didn't want to do, for example, using resources to collect data on items that they didn't care about or in areas where they already knew what they wanted to do. It's an interesting issue—having to calibrate what you're offering to the capacities of the people who are receiving it.

Evaluator 3: And offering both time and skills.

Evaluator 1: I think this notion of technical assistance and how much choice projects have in the use of this assistance pervades all of the programs in different ways.

Evaluator 4: So one dimension is the amount of choice they have.

Evaluator 2: How do we broaden the group that can be facilitated—the group in the middle zone? In my opinion technical assistance is where it's at. How do we expand that window of people who actually want to engage and use this effectively?

Evaluator 4: If we think about it in terms of capacity being one variable, the power of figuring what people need to do anyway and helping them do it more easily. . . Basically nobody wants to have more work made for them. I think to the extent that they perceive, as we did originally, that participating with you would satisfy NSF, then they might do it.

Evaluator 1: Unfortunately, in our experience, our time is wasted and our input ignored if a project has sought our assistance only because NSF told them to do so. But—however, if we'd been able to identify things that they perceived as helping them do their jobs better and more efficiently, they might have valued our assistance much more.

Lesson 4

A multisite evaluator plays the role of buffer between the funder and project staff and needs to maintain open and ethical relationships.

NEW DIRECTIONS FOR EVALUATION • DOI: 10.1002/ev

Speaking as multisite program evaluators, each of the evaluators who oversaw large-scale program evaluations served two masters, and they noted the important role they played as buffers between NSF staff and project staff whom NSF had funded. The program evaluators learned firsthand the issues that affected specific projects and could speak uniquely to NSF about the projects' collective concerns and needs. Because the evaluators reported to the funder (not to individual projects), they were free to report these concerns honestly and openly, but they emphasized the significance of never betraying people's trust. Ethical behavior must overshadow every action, regardless of its possible consequences.

> Evaluator 1: I did see part of my role as a buffer. As the program evaluator, I could speak on behalf of the projects, and I had a stronger voice than each of the projects individually.

> Evaluator 4: That's really interesting because the same thing happened with the SSIs [Statewide Systemic Initiatives] and monitors. They saw themselves as the buffer—the sanity—to represent the projects when project staff thought NSF was being arbitrary.

> Evaluator 2: Much of the power of what we do comes from what I would call semiprivate channels where we talk with funders quite directly. When they ask how things are going, you can choose what you talk about. Funders also trust you in a way. They make their own decisions reading the reports, but there's a second source of data that's saying, "Evaluator, what rose to the top for you? What things should we attend to?"

> Evaluator 4: But this can go too far. When a program officer asked me about which project was doing a good job, I said, "Either I'm evaluating them, in which case it's unethical for me to tell you, or I'm not evaluating them, and I don't have a clue." Then he said, "Well, what are you hearing?" I said, "Great. Program evaluation by innuendo. . ."

> Evaluator 2: Another principle of this buffer role would be to honor confidences. If you can't keep things confidential, you shouldn't be in the business. You can help the funder understand what's going on without "narc-ing" on the projects. If you tell somebody stuff out of that realm, expect them to get burned.

> Evaluator 4: They'll never trust you again.

> Evaluator 2: Keeping your integrity. I think it's real easy to sell your integrity. It comes down to either keeping your word or not, and the time that you don't keep your word is when you're no longer good for anything. People keep hiring me, and in part they keep hiring me because they know they can trust me.

> Evaluator 4: We've chosen long-term over short-term, but it ain't easy. I know a lot of evaluators who pull their punches. The fact that we were all funded

NEW DIRECTIONS FOR EVALUATION • DOI: 10.1002/ev

directly from NSF as opposed to the projects actually made it easier, to be honest, because usually you report to a PI, and they can cut you out at any point.

Evaluator 1: That's true. That's a good point.

Evaluator 4: What's unique is nimbleness in terms of keeping confidences. You're essentially serving two masters, and if you forget that, you're going to crash and burn. You can't take the project's side and ignore NSF's legitimate needs. Nor can you ignore the project's realities in feeding information to NSF. You're like a broker, and what we're saying is be an honest broker.

Evaluator 2: You have to know the stakeholders. It comes down to knowing your stakeholders and serving your stakeholders ethically.

Lesson 5

Multisite evaluators should always raise cultural issues for consideration.

The past decade has witnessed the ascent of cultural concerns as central to high-quality evaluation practice. During an Advisory Committee meeting for this research project, Karen Kirkhart asked why cultural issues were not more present in the discussion of the four evaluations. In reflecting on her comments, the group came to a conclusion that holds the potential to change multisite evaluation practice.

Evaluator 4: We had data in our evaluation that could have shed light on some cultural issues, but no one asked us to, and we didn't think of it ourselves. For example, we didn't compute the percentage of teachers in the program, whether the rate of participation was equally high for teachers in high-poverty schools. We could have, but we didn't.

Evaluator 1: Or another question might have been: Did a representative proportion of teachers of color participate?

Evaluator 4: That was not put into an evaluation question. It was not on anyone's radar screen. It *was* on the radar screen of the projects, and it was on the radar of NSF in seeking high-needs districts.

Evaluator 1: Right. They only funded places that were high needs.

Evaluator 4: Well, not always, but disproportionately. There were more minority kids, and we did report that. How did the distribution in the students' participating districts compare to the nation as a whole? But we didn't look within the participating districts, once selected, to see if there was more or less involvement because there was no one bringing those questions to the fore.

Facilitator: It wasn't a stakeholder issue in that sense, except for society in the broadest sense?

NEW DIRECTIONS FOR EVALUATION • DOI: 10.1002/ev

Evaluator 4: There were very few participants or PIs of color. In my experience, when people of color are at the table, cultural concerns are more likely to be at the forefront of discussion. But, for whatever reason, the national evaluations weren't asking those questions outright, the projects weren't always asking those questions, and we didn't think of it either. Certainly in retrospect we had brought in cultural concerns. We can't let ourselves off the hook because the stakeholders did not bring up these issues. It's an interesting question: If the client didn't have questions about differential impact, are we ethically, morally obligated to bring that to their attention?

Evaluator 1: Jennifer Greene links her new model, educated, value-engaged evaluation, to STEM [science, technology, engineering, and mathematics] evaluations specifically because of NSF's interest in broadening participation. We're not going to broaden participation unless this sort of equity is at the core of our concern. Does the program provide for all people the same sorts of valued experience?

Evaluator 4: I would say if that was at the core, then it's the client's responsibility to put it in as a question. I actually think it would be evaluation malpractice to put resources into things that are not answering the client's questions.

Evaluator 2: To me that's the kind of question that's being posed: Should or must we take on culture as a component of the evaluation in every job?

Evaluator 4: You mean that you're not doing a good job unless you do it?

Evaluator 2: Right. If you don't address culture, you're not doing a good job.

Evaluator 4: If a client doesn't tell me to do a Bonferroni adjustment, I may still do something like that because I know that one needs to do that. Is addressing culture like the Bonferroni adjustment?

Evaluator 2: I'd like to phrase that a little bit differently and say as an evaluator you certainly can and probably should open the door or at some point say, "You've not attended to these kinds of issues."

Evaluator 4: So you're asking the client to clarify "to what extent are you interested in looking at the impact of this program on . . .?" I would agree with that.

Facilitator: And if they say, "No, I'm not interested"?

Evaluator 4: Then, you're not God. It's their resources. I would go this far with the cultural issue. I think that in multisite evaluation it is the evaluator's responsibility. The evaluator could be helped by having a checklist of potential disaggregations to bring to the attention of the client and identify any subgroups that they are particularly interested in looking at. I'm not God so I don't tell them they have to be interested. I just want to make sure they've had the opportunity to consider what it might get them and what it might cost them to do that.

NEW DIRECTIONS FOR EVALUATION • DOI: 10.1002/ev

Evaluator 2: I think it's incumbent on us to address cultural aspects whether or not the client wants them addressed—it is something that responsible professionals feel they must do.

Evaluator 4: I would agree with you that if the client doesn't ask for it, that's not enough. Putting it in front of the client and making the case that it might matter is really about as far as I think we can go. But I worry that it will subvert the entire evaluation by becoming formulaic. If you are saying one of the things we want to look at is differential effects, how do we look at it? That's what I'm thinking about. There are these kinds of indicators of sensing, and at the very least we should elevate them. I would say that this is not just cultural; it is populations—subgroups that you might want to look at.

Evaluator 2: How you come at it, how well you do it, how much you do it—it varies by situation.

Evaluator 4: But you at least should consider it.

Evaluator 2: Yes, it's always on that table and it should be on the table.

Lesson 6

There are no perfect evaluations, multisite or otherwise, and evaluators should simply accept that fact.

The final lesson applies not just to multisite evaluations, but to all evaluation practice. These seasoned professionals highlighted the situational nature of program evaluation and the challenge evaluators face in completing studies given the constraints present in any evaluation setting.

Evaluator 4: Every time we would have plans, someone would point out a flaw. I said, "Can we just acknowledge that this is going to be flawed no matter what we do and that we're trying to decide which flaw we can live with? If you're going to veto an idea because it has a flaw, I'm leaving because everything has a flaw."

Evaluator 2: I was recently reminded of one of the most important lessons from one of my first evaluations. The PI had an evaluation project with NSF and had come to the meetings, and we had to do this survey work. My colleague and I would always say, "But we can't get this done in this time," and we'd always have reasons why it couldn't be done on time. Finally, the PI said, "I've had enough of this. This thing has to be done by this date. It *will* be done by this date. We know there are going to be problems with it, but we're going to get it done." So we did it. But up until that point there were a thousand reasons why it just couldn't happen. There were all these excuses, or not excuses, but good reasons, why things couldn't be done exactly right.

Evaluator 4: Right—there is no perfect in social science, so get over it and move on.

Evaluator 1: Or at least document the limitations.

Evaluator 4: You have to understand what you're trading off and have a ratio-nale for why you choose which of the less-than-perfect situations you choose . . .

Taken together, the four participants in the Chapel Hill conversation had over 100 years of evaluation experience. The lessons they came to over the course of a day of discussion point to the following recommendations for multisite evaluation practice:

1. Retain control of decisions regarding both evaluation design and instru-mentation, even as you involve people in multiple ways to build own-ership.
2. Thoughtfully use the evaluation process and its outcomes as interven-tions to improve individual projects.
3. Provide support to the extent possible for project staff to complete eval-uation tasks, both to ensure high-quality data and to increase project ownership of the evaluation.
4. Purposefully and openly serve as a buffer between the funder and proj-ect staff, acting at all times ethically.
5. Take leadership in raising cultural issues for people's consideration dur-ing the planning and implementation of the program evaluation.
6. Design and conduct the best evaluations possible, documenting limi-tations and being fully aware of trade-offs and necessary compromises.

It is likely that few evaluators to date have been formally trained to con-duct multisite evaluations, and this wisdom from four evaluation elders begins an ongoing conversation about this special form of practice.

JEAN A. KING is a professor and director of graduate studies in the Department of Organizational Leadership, Policy, and Development at the University of Minnesota.

PATRICIA A. ROSS is a doctoral student in the Department of Educational Psy-chology at the University of Minnesota.

CATHERINE CALLOW-HEUSSER is president of EndVision Research and Evalua-tion, LLC, in Logan, Utah, and previously served as principal investigator on an NSF Mathematics–Science Partnership Research, Evaluation, and Technical Assistance Grant at Utah State University.

NEW DIRECTIONS FOR EVALUATION • DOI: 10.1002/ev

Arlen R. Gullickson *is an emeritus professor at Western Michigan University (WMU) and director of Evalua|t|e, an NSF-funded evaluation resource center housed in The Evaluation Center at WMU for the Advanced Technological Education program.*

Frances Lawrenz *is the Wallace Professor of Teaching and Learning in the Department of Educational Psychology and the associate vice president for research at the University of Minnesota.*

Iris R. Weiss *is president of Horizon Research, Inc., a contract research firm in Chapel Hill, North Carolina, specializing in research and evaluation in science and mathematics education.*

New Directions for Evaluation • DOI: 10.1002/ev

Kirkhart, K. E. (2011). Culture and influence in multisite evaluation. In J. A. King & F. Lawrenz (Eds.), *Multisite evaluation practice: Lessons and reflections from four cases. New Directions for Evaluation, 129*, 73–85.

8

Culture and Influence in Multisite Evaluation

Karen E. Kirkhart

Abstract

Understanding the influence of multisite evaluation requires careful consideration of cultural context. The author illustrates dimensions of influence and culture with excerpts from four National Science Foundation evaluation case studies and summarizes what influence teaches us about culture and what culture teaches us about influence. © Wiley Periodicals, Inc., and the American Evaluation Association.

The intention to go "Beyond Evaluation Use" (see "Editors' Notes," this issue) that underpins the recent collaboration of Lawrenz and King is important on many levels. It takes us beyond intended users to examine the impact of evaluation on what may be considered secondary audiences, and it draws us into a deeper examination of what constitutes involvement and influence. The context of multisite evaluation immediately signals the complexity of inquiry on influence, serving as a cautionary warning to avoid simple conclusions. Against this backdrop is the puzzling fact that although culture has been increasingly recognized as central to evaluation theory and practice, culture has been virtually invisible in studies of evaluation influence. This chapter seeks to address that omission. The basic premise of this chapter is that *evaluation influence must be understood and studied as a cultural phenomenon*. Nowhere is this truer than in multisite evaluation.

All evaluation occurs in contexts infused with culture; there is no such thing as "culture-free" evaluation. It follows that all evaluators implicitly work with culture; however, not all do so mindfully. When we are not attentive to culture, our assumptions are implicitly grounded in majority perspectives—for example, white, heterosexual, middle class, able bodied— that position culture as something different, "special," foreign, or distant. Rather than viewing culture as something "out there," it is important to examine the ways in which it's "in here"—in the sites of our work, the theories to which we subscribe, the methods we employ, and the differences we seek to make through our evaluations.

To examine the particular intersection of culture and evaluation influence, this chapter offers some definitions and conceptual frameworks, and then moves to lessons learned from thinking about culture in the sites of Beyond Evaluation Use. Concluding comments underscore the importance of making culture visible in our conversations, explorations, and evaluation practices that support influence.

Dimensions of Influence

Beyond Evaluation Use draws upon Kirkhart's (2000) Integrated Theory of Influence (ITI), which assumes an inclusive definition of evaluation influence—the capacity to produce effects on others through intangible or indirect means.[1] Beyond Evaluation Use addresses all three ITI dimensions of influence—source, intention, and time—albeit to varying degrees.

Source

Source refers to the aspect of evaluation that exerts influence. Evaluation influences systems through both the results of inquiry and the inquiry process itself. Beyond Evaluation Use explores the impact of evaluation generated by both sources. Process-based influence (also referred to as process use; Patton, 2008) refers to impact that emanates from conducting evaluation, extending the scope of influence to evaluation implementation. Participation (cast as *involvement* in Beyond Evaluation Use) in the evaluation process affects stakeholders. The Local Systemic Change through Teacher Enhancement (LSC) evaluation offers a clear example of process-based influence. LSC sets high standards of rigor in its instrument development and evaluation. These standards influenced how project leaders and evaluators thought about inquiry, increased critical thinking about what Scriven (1991) calls "ritualized" evaluation—evaluation done for the sake of doing it—and developed an appreciation that not all inquiry was good.

Results-based influence focuses attention on evaluation findings. For example, in the Advanced Technological Education (ATE) program, data from the Web-based survey reportedly gave projects a broader perspective and helped them to move ahead, and the data from the 13 site visits were subsequently presented as nine issue papers (Lawrenz, Gullickson, & Toal, 2007). Note that process and results as sources of influence may occur in combination. For example, LSC reported solid results-based influence as well as the previously cited process-based influence. Project principal investigators used the program evaluation findings to meet contractual arrangements, develop future plans, and make changes to their projects.

Intention

Intention refers to how closely the observed influence conforms to anticipated pathways and desired impacts. Beyond Evaluation Use addresses both intended and unintended influence. Intended influence is illustrated by the Math Science Partnership–Research, Technical Assistance and Evaluation (MSP-RETA) Capacity Building Initiative at Utah State University. MSP-RETA provided technical assistance and instruction to support the evaluation capacity of MSP projects, so the influence of the RETA process was clearly intentional.

Unintended influence refers to unanticipated users, pathways, or directions of impact. To the extent that the National Science Foundation (NSF) was the original intended user of the core-evaluation information, the project-level focus of Beyond Evaluation Use positions it as study of influence on unintended users. Unintended influence may be positive or negative. Positive examples of unintended influence of core evaluations at the project level are visible in ATE, LSC, and the Collaboratives for Excellence in Teacher Preparation (CETP); however, not all unintended influence is positive. In LSC, the timing of the core evaluation increased workload and costs, reportedly impinging on the projects' local evaluation activities.

Time

Time refers to when influence occurs. Though time is continuous, it may be particularly fruitful to notice influence concurrent with the evaluation (immediate), at a point of closure (end of cycle), and after the evaluation has concluded (long-term) (Kirkhart, 2000). In Beyond Evaluation Use, time is visible in the life cycle of each of these programs, its relationship to the core evaluation (or technical assistance), and to NSF funding. Beyond Evaluation Use is uniquely well positioned to reflect on long-term influence, because it addresses programs with extended funding and evaluation experience. Immediate influence is illustrated by MSP-RETA, in which impact unfolded concurrent with the technical assistance. End-of-cycle influence is visible in the use of data from ATE's annual Web-based survey.

Not only do the dimensions of source, intention, and time provide a framework for mapping evaluation influence, but they also support reflections on culture.

NEW DIRECTIONS FOR EVALUATION • DOI: 10.1002/ev

Dimensions of Culture

Culture is a complex construct. Although many definitions exist, commonalities include the idea of culture representing shared norms, values, and assumptions that are learned and passed on from one generation or cohort to another (Barnouw, 1985; Schein, 1996). Culture involves taken-for-granted, often tacit ways of perceiving, thinking, and reacting. Although cultural terrain is often marked by descriptors such as race, ethnicity, language, social class, religion, gender, sexual orientation, disability, age, immigration status, or geographic location, it is important not to *equate* culture with fixed categories (Pon, 2009; Sakamoto, 2007). Rather than adopt an absolute definition of culture, the task is to appreciate the complexity of its meaning in a specific context.

Culture enters evaluation both from the individuals who participate and through the organizations and institutions of which they are a part. Though this section considers each perspective in turn, they are in fact intertwined, as discussed below.

Culture From an Individual Perspective

Each of us as an individual simultaneously holds multiple cultural identifications that are fluid in several ways (Ridley, Mendoza, Kanitz, Angermeier, & Zenk, 1994). The personal meaning attached to a given identification may shift in salience or substance as an individual moves from one context to another or developmentally through the life cycle. When a group of individuals share a common identification, there are other identifications or unique personal meanings that are not shared, erasing the notion of absolute cultural categories. Nevertheless, categorical labels are often used to organize cultural information, and evaluators must be aware of how differential power and privilege become attached to such descriptors.

Each evaluator brings a unique mix of individual cultural identifications into his/her work. Jean King, one of the principal investigators of Beyond Evaluation Use, speaks of her position as "a white, middle-class, privileged evaluator" and describes how her values of empiricism, persistence, and *tikkun olam* (healing the world) were passed down from her science teacher father (King, 2004). Few such personal identifications are visible in the four cases themselves. An LSC project report noted, "LSC-treated teachers taught approximately 70,000 students, approximately half of whom were from minority groups" (Johnson & Greenseid, 2007, p. 6). It is unclear what diversity dimensions—economic, linguistic, ethnic, ability—are reflected in the "minority" designation, but it does signal the presence of cultural diversity that merits exploration.

Culture From an Organizational Perspective

Despite exhortations more than a decade ago (Schein, 1996), the organizational side of culture has not been well integrated into the literature on culturally competent professional practice, including the practice of evaluation. When cultural competence is cited as necessary in evaluation (for example, American Evaluation Association, 2004; King, Stevahn, Ghere, & Minnema, 2001; SenGupta, Hopson, & Thompson-Robinson, 2004), it is often illustrated with reference to individual characteristics.

Organizations and institutions reflect their own values, assumptions, and knowledge bases that define organizational culture along dimensions such as disciplinary background, occupational norms, job descriptions, or role requirements. Here again, culture is situation specific (Balthasar, 2009). Manifestations of culture from an organizational perspective include "cultural forms (such as rituals, organizational stories, jargon, humor, and physical arrangements), formal practices (such as pay schemes and hierarchical reporting structures), informal practices (such as norms) and content themes [such as beliefs, assumptions, or values]" (Martin, 2002, pp. 64–65). Culture both supports and constrains the behavior of members of an organization or institution.

Beyond Evaluation Use offers glimpses of the organizational identifications that shape the context of these cases. LSC describes its project locations in terms of urban, suburban, small city, and rural; CETP identifies the types of organizations that engaged as collaborators—higher education institutions, school districts, businesses, and state departments of education; MSP names at least some of its corporate partners; ATE centers require a regional or national focus, not purely a local one. Each of these settings speaks to the organizational cultures that shape these programs.

Putting Culture in Context

Figure 8.1 visually portrays the dual ways in which culture enters both the context of evaluation operation and implementation (the territory of process-based influence) and the context of information dissemination and action (the territory of results-based influence). Micro and macro considerations of culture are intertwined. The intersection indicates that the salience

Figure 8.1. Complexities of Culture: Individual and Organizational Perspectives, Grounded in Context

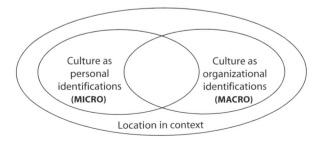

of individual cultural identifications is shaped by cultural context and that diversity within organizational culture is shaped by individual members. This intersection is explicit in Beyond Evaluation Use. "Participants" were defined not as individual people but as individual projects; however, data were collected from individual people serving as representatives of their projects. These respondents bring to the table both their individual cultural backgrounds and that of their project context.

Although this visual is helpful in juxtaposing micro and macro perspectives, the image is also potentially misleading and inaccurate, so three caveats must follow. First, the image in Figure 8.1 is too tidy. Culture is messy and complicated, not subject to clean, absolutist definitions. The borders of cultural identifications are permeable and fluid, stirred by multiple intersecting identifications. This leads to the second major inaccuracy of Figure 8.1: Dimensions of culture appear static. In truth, they are fluid and dynamic, continuously in motion, responding to context (Este, 2007). The micro- and macroelements shift in shape and salience (size), but they never lose their connection. Third, the boundaries between culture and context are themselves permeable (Martin, 2002). Ideas and meanings may be imported or exported from the individual or organization to the larger community or surrounding social context, refreshing and reinventing cultural identifications.

How Shall We Think About Culture in Multisite Evaluation?

Although this configuration exists within any given context, the contexts of evaluation are multiple, not singular. To appreciate culture in multisite evaluation requires attention to multiple cultural locations. Figure 8.2 depicts the contexts named in Beyond Evaluation Use.[2] In this multisite evaluation, culture moves from local sites of a given project, to the sites of projects themselves, to the four programs that are represented in this issue, to NSF

Figure 8.2. Representations of Culture Across Sites

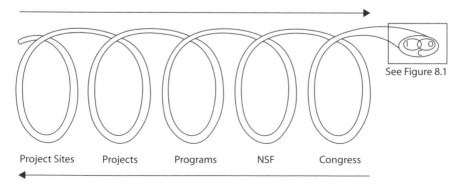

See Figure 8.1

Project Sites   Projects   Programs   NSF   Congress

as a site, responsive to Congress as a stakeholder site. These are all sites of influence—intended or unintended—within which culture can be reflected upon.

Figure 8.2 depicts these sites horizontally rather than vertically to avoid portraying a hierarchy in which one context is privileged over another. The lateral arrows above and below the spiral indicate influence moving across these sites in both directions. The cross-sectional view at the right reminds us that context is dimensional and infused with culture bubbling as a micro–macro mix across these interconnected sites.

As program funder and primary client of the three evaluations and one technical assistance initiative, NSF itself is a major site of influence, though its use is not the subject of Beyond Evaluation Use. The spiral of influence from NSF to project sites is specific to each of the cases. For CETP, *program* refers to the collection of CETP projects; *projects* refers to local collaboratives at 19 locations around the country; *project sites* represent specific organizations participating in each collaboration, each of which brings its own distinct cultural mix to the table. Projects are characterized as "mature" (3 years or more of funding) and "developing," but little else is known about these evaluands. Stage of program development is a limited marker of organizational culture.

LSC illustrates the flexibility of the "loops" in the coiling spiral of Figure 8.2. As drawn, the LSC *program* refers to Local Systemic Change for Teacher Enhancement, under which 88 *projects* were funded, encompassing 4,000 schools as *project sites*. However, these sites spanned 31 states and 476 districts, each of which could be represented as its own site, adding loops in the coil as visual markers between projects and project (school) sites.

Making Culture Visible: Lessons Learned

Recognizing culture as an integral component of evaluation influence enriches the understanding of both culture and influence. This section examines each direction of their reciprocal relationship.

What Does Influence Teach Us About Culture?

Location, location, location. Perhaps nowhere in the evaluation literature does the importance of context come across more clearly and consistently than in the literature on utilization. The multiple sites of Beyond Evaluation Use underscore the fluidity of culture as it is defined and reinvented at different levels of a system. Multisite work specifically reminds evaluators to consider different locations of culture in their work, even when working primarily in one project or program. All culture is local in the sense that one must always consider it with fresh eyes as one moves across contexts and locations. For example, the "perceived quality of the evaluator" theme cited in the cross-case analysis mixes credibility of the evaluator with perceived quality of the evaluation, both of which may be context-specific judgments. What enhances evaluator credibility in one context (for example, speaking a language other than English) may be irrelevant in a second context or actually undermine credibility in a third. The same argument applies to the perceived quality of an evaluation. A particular evaluation design (for example, a randomized controlled experiment) may strengthen validity in one context, be irrelevant to a second (for example, where evaluation questions do not focus on causal impact), and threaten validity in a third (Johnson, Kirkhart, Madison, Noley, & Solano-Flores, 2008).

Culture is personal. From the earliest empirical examination of use (Patton et al., 1977) to this present study, the "personal factor" shines through as a key determinant of evaluation influence. What gives an evaluator the credibility to exert influence in a particular context goes beyond credentials and evaluation expertise to include life experience, knowledge of cultural context, and interpersonal skills. It is noteworthy to see that even in a large multisite study where the details of local context are not very visible, the "personal factor" emerges from the interview data to remind us not to lose sight of individuals and relationships. For example, in the CETP case study, Lawrenz was already deeply familiar with CETP in her role as principal investigator of their core evaluation prior to beginning Beyond Evaluation Use. Her personal experience and relationships with project sites plus her respect for and appreciation of their efforts and their practice contexts supported both involvement and influence.

Power and agenda setting. The intention dimension of influence leads importantly to asking, "*Whose* intention?" and examining the power relationships surrounding the answers. This is a very useful reminder that evaluation does not occupy a neutral space with respect to culture.

The issue of who sets the agenda for an evaluation is a fundamental issue that crosses evaluation models, often marking a point of tension. In Beyond Evaluation Use, power was visible in the amount of control that local projects had over their involvement in the multisite evaluation. Despite the multisite evaluation's emphasis on partnership and collaboration, both NSF and Beyond Evaluation Use invoked the authority of their positions to gain involvement. ATE was arguably the most evaluator-directed program; that is, it involved the least local control and most explicit use of NSF authority to facilitate data collection. Though survey completion was reportedly not required, NSF's "clear expectation" was communicated, plus the names of nonrespondents were collected, restricting the projects' degrees of freedom and challenging the voluntary nature of participation.

Culture resists operationalization. Like influence, the whole of culture as a construct is greater than the sum of its individual parts. Culture cannot be reduced to methods and procedures alone—for example, performing subgroup analyses by gender, ethnicity, or economic markers—though such analyses may provide useful pieces of a larger puzzle. Cultural boundaries are permeable, fluctuating, and ambiguous (Martin, 2002). Evaluators must engage culture in multiple ways and approach operationalizations of culture with humility; there are many ways to misunderstand. Beyond Evaluation Use employed multiple methods of inquiry—site visits, direct observation, written reflection, archival review, interview, and survey. Although none of these was directed explicitly at culture in the current study, mixed methods support multivocal understandings and help evaluators resist getting locked into a single perspective.

What Does Culture Teach Us About Influence?

Avoid dichotomous thinking. Much of the literature on culture—especially that coming from critical theory—concerns the deconstruction of categories traditionally used to name culture. This is done by closer reflection on the diversity within cultural categories (for example, race/ethnicity or immigration history), by redefining binary categories as multiplicities and continua (for example, gender identification and sexual orientation—see Fausto-Sterling, 1993; Gergen, 1993), and by emphasizing the multiple overlapping cultural identifications that create unique meaning (Ridley et al., 1994). Cultural membership is a matter of intensity rather than a member/nonmember dichotomy (Martin, 2002). Thus, what is learned about influence concerns the importance of troubling the boundaries of dichotomous categories. Though Kirkhart (2000) explicitly noted, "source, intention, and time may be more accurately characterized as continua, reflecting gray areas that fall between the levels" (p. 8), the designations within each dimension have perhaps carried too much weight. Intention, for example, is shown in this inquiry to be a matter of degree rather than an absolute status. The cross-case analysis characterizes the users examined as "somewhat unintended," indicating that although they were not previously considered primary users, as was NSF, neither were they completely outside the scope of NSF's intended influence.

Ownership and autonomy. Western evaluation typically makes the assumption that dissemination of results is a desirable strategy to improve programs and to better the human condition. Too often, studies of influence do not stop to examine this assumption. Culture leads us to reflect on issues of power and ownership, of self-determination and autonomy, and of proprietary knowledge that is not intended to be exported or shared. Culture also leads us to notice whose agendas are being served and whose interests are ignored or impeded when evaluation exerts influence. This is illustrated by indigenous epistemology's strong challenge to colonization and appropriation (Crazy Bull, 1997; LaFrance, 2004; Smith, 1999), and it is also visible in organizational culture and leadership (Martin, 2002; Schein, 2004).

In the present study, the agendas of the four programs were clear, set by the terms of their funding. Despite efforts to create ownership at the project level, the extent to which this was achieved is often unclear. For example,

LSC sought to respect the unique characteristics of the sites and build in local adaptation to their design, permitting sites to add elements to their data set. Nevertheless, when LSC evaluators describe their involvement as "doing what we were supposed to do," it suggests that such strategies may be insufficient to create a true sense of ownership and raises questions about meaningful engagement when the primary agenda has been externally determined.

Importance of consequences. Culture teaches us to notice the consequences of evaluation influence and how such consequences relate to broader issues of equity and social justice. This speaks both to the consequences of what was included in a given evaluation and the consequences of what was omitted that, in the words of Milner (2007), may lead to "dangers seen, unseen, and unforeseen." Culture cautions us to temper our understanding of the apparent success of our evaluation implementation (process-based influence) and our dissemination/utilization efforts (results-based influence) with a careful reflection on consequences. It is important that evaluation not unintentionally disrupt the programs that it seeks to support, nor replicate past oppression by silencing important voices. One wonders, for example, how the views of the parents, named as stakeholders in the MSP-RETA case study, may have differed from those of the teachers and administrators. Moreover, one evaluation may have consequences that impact another. In the complex terrain of multisite evaluation, the probability grows. Lawrenz et al. (this issue) allude to this point in the cross-case analysis when they note evidence of tensions in all four cases between the overall evaluation and the local projects and their evaluation efforts.

Importance of history. Culture draws attention to historically relevant information, extending the time frame of influence. Current theories position the chronology of influence around the time frame of the evaluation, looking for impact that emerges concurrent with the evaluation, at the conclusion of the evaluation or beyond. Hall (2004) extends the time frame to include influence emanating from evaluation anticipation, before any actual decision to evaluate is made. His call for a cultural analysis of influence suggests something even more expansive: To appreciate and to interpret the influence surrounding a given study or group of studies correctly requires historical understanding of the context, the evaluand, and the values and traditions that intersect these. This may extend the relevant time frame by decades or even generations/life cycles when one is seeking to appreciate the cultural significance of evaluation. Lawrenz et al. (this issue) speak of the life cycles of both individuals and projects in the cross-case analysis. The significance of prior history with evaluation itself, for example, is clearly visible in the CETP case study, where multiple prior internal and external evaluations stood in different relationships to the collaboratives— from project-level evaluation, to the initial external evaluation that was not deemed useful, to the core evaluation that served as evaluand for the Beyond Evaluation Use evaluation. Projects' response to requests for involvement in Beyond Evaluation Use must be understood in this historical context.

NEW DIRECTIONS FOR EVALUATION • DOI: 10.1002/ev

Conclusion

This chapter has argued that raising the visibility of culture is necessary for a full and complete appreciation of evaluation influence beyond a narrow interpretation of use. Thoughtful inclusion of individual and organizational aspects of culture supports valid understanding of evaluation influence and of factors such as involvement that support influence.

Multisite evaluation offers a particularly rich opportunity to reflect on culture, yet culture is often rendered invisible in cross-site aggregation. It is important to resist the elision of culture from multisite studies, particularly from studies of influence. The meaning of influence as a construct must be understood and represented within cultural context. If culture is omitted, the construct of influence is underrepresented, which in turn undermines validity arguments (Kane, 2006; Messick, 1995).

Beyond the influence of specific findings or of the process as it impacts those involved at a given site, there is the influence produced by the cumulative impact of the questions raised. Apart from site-specific culture-based analyses or interpretations, the fact that evaluations raise questions about culture is significant. For multisite studies, it is important to see equity and social justice as issues suitable for cross-site synthesis; for example, exploring issues of access to services that break along cultural identifications or understanding how differential outcomes are affected by cultural context. Such inclusion of culture lays a foundation for multisite evaluations to take an antioppressive stance, raising issues of social justice for reflection and discussion. This does not presume an advocacy paradigm of evaluation. Evaluation can make visible important issues of equity and justice simply by raising questions and bringing them into public and professional awareness as legitimate concerns worthy of discussion. The wide-angle lens of multisite evaluation has the power to bring culture into focus for our profession.

Notes

1. Note that *all* influence may be considered *indirect* in the sense that it is mediated through multiple mechanisms and pathways (Henry & Mark, 2003). Even instrumental results-based use that we refer to as "direct" travels individual, interpersonal, and collective pathways from information to action. The Mark and Henry (2004) work formed another of the theory bases of Beyond Evaluation Use.
2. The graphic design in Figure 8.2 was created by Jennifer L. Browning, Brooklyn, NY.

References

American Evaluation Association. (2004). *Guiding principles for evaluators.* Retrieved from http://www.eval.org/GPTraining/GPTrainingOverview.asp

Balthasar, A. (2009). Institutional design and utilization of evaluation: A contribution to a theory of evaluation influence based on Swiss experience. *Evaluation Review, 33*(3), 226–256.

Barnouw, V. (1985). *Culture and personality* (4th ed.). Homewood, IL: The Dorsey Press.

Crazy Bull, C. (1997). A native conversation about research and scholarship. *Tribal College Journal, 9*, 17–23.

Este, D. (2007). Cultural competency and social work practice in Canada: A retrospective examination. *Canadian Social Work Review, 24*(1), 93–104.

Fausto-Sterling, A. (1993, March/April). The five sexes: Why male and female are not enough. *The Sciences*, 20–24. Retrieved from: http://frank.mtsu.edu/~phollowa/5sexes.html

Gergen, M. (1993). Unbundling our binaries—Genders, sexualities, desires. In S. Wilkinson & C. Kitzinger (Eds.), *Heterosexuality: A feminism & psychology reader* (pp. 62–64). Newbury Park, CA: Sage.

Hall, M. E. (2004, November). *Persuasive language, responsive design: Towards broader evaluation utilization.* In K. E. Kirkhart (Chair), What is the nature of evaluation use/influence? Panel at the annual meeting of the American Evaluation Association, Atlanta, GA.

Henry, G. T., & Mark, M. M. (2003). Beyond evaluation use: Understanding evaluation's influence on attitudes and actions. *American Journal of Evaluation, 24*(3), 293–314.

Johnson, E. C., Kirkhart, K. E., Madison, A. M., Noley, G. B., & Solano-Flores, G. (2008). The impact of narrow views of scientific rigor on evaluation practices for underrepresented groups. In N. L. Smith & P. R. Brandon (Eds.), *Fundamental issues in evaluation* (pp. 197–218). New York: Guilford.

Johnson, K., & Greenseid, L. (2007). A case study of the impact of the Local Systemic Change through Teacher Enhancement (LSC) core evaluation (Report 3. Beyond evaluation use: Determining the effect of participation on the influence of NSF program evaluations). Minneapolis: University of Minnesota College of Education and Human Development.

Kane, M. T. (2006). Validation. In R. Brennan (Ed.), *Educational measurement* (4th ed., pp. 17–64). Westport, CT: American Council on Education and Praeger.

King, J. A. (2004). *Tikkun olam*: The roots of participatory evaluation. In M. C. Alkin (Ed.), *Evaluation roots: Tracing theorists' views and influences* (pp. 331–342). Thousand Oaks, CA: Sage.

King, J. A., Stevahn, L., Ghere, G., & Minnema, J. (2001). Toward a taxonomy of essential program evaluator competencies. *American Journal of Evaluation, 22*(2), 229–247.

Kirkhart, K. E. (2000). Reconceptualizing evaluation use: An integrated theory of influence. In V. J. Caracelli & H. Preskill (Eds.), *The expanding scope of evaluation use. New Directions for Evaluation, 88*, 5–23.

LaFrance, J. (2004). Culturally competent evaluation in Indian Country. In M. Thompson-Robinson, R. Hopson, & S. SenGupta (Eds.), *In search of cultural competence in evaluation: Toward principles and practices. New Directions for Evaluation, 102*, 39–50.

Lawrenz, F., Gullickson, A., & Toal, S. (2007). Dissemination: Handmaiden to evaluation use. *American Journal of Evaluation, 28*(3), 275–289.

Mark, M. M., & Henry, G. T. (2004). The mechanisms and outcomes of evaluation influence. *Evaluation, 10*, 35–57.

Martin, J. (2002). *Organizational culture: Mapping the terrain*. Thousand Oaks, CA: Sage.

Messick, S. (1995). Validity of psychological assessment: Validation of inferences from persons' responses and performance as scientific inquiry into score meaning. *American Psychologist, 50*, 741–749.

Milner, H. R. (2007). Race, culture, and researcher positionality: Working through dangers seen, unseen, and unforeseen. *Educational Researcher, 36*(7), 388–400.

Patton, M. Q. (2008). *Utilization-focused evaluation* (4th ed.) Thousand Oaks, CA: Sage.

Patton, M. Q., Grimes, P. S., Guthrie, K. M., Brennan, N. J., French, B. D., & Blyth, D. A. (1977). In search of impact: An analysis of the utilization of federal health evaluation research. In C. H. Weiss (Ed.), *Using social research in public policy making* (pp. 141–164). Lexington, MA: D. C. Heath.

Pon, G. (2009). Cultural competency as new racism: An ontology of forgetting. *Journal of Progressive Human Services, 20*(1), 59–71.

Ridley, C. R., Mendoza, D. W., Kanitz, B. E., Angermeier, L., & Zenk, R. (1994). Cultural sensitivity in multicultural counseling: A perceptual schema model. *Journal of Counseling Psychology, 41*(2), 125–136.

Sakamoto, I. (2007). An anti-oppressive approach to cultural competence. *Canadian Social Work Review, 24*(1), 105–114.

Schein, E. H. (1996). Culture: The missing concept in organizational studies. *Administrative Science Quarterly, 41,* 229–240.

Schein, E. H. (2004). *Organizational culture and leadership.* San Francisco: Jossey-Bass.

Scriven, M. (1991). *Evaluation thesaurus* (4th ed.). Newbury Park, CA: Sage.

SenGupta, S., Hopson, R., & Thompson-Robinson, M. (2004). Cultural competence in evaluation. An overview. In M. Thompson-Robinson, R. Hopson, & S. SenGupta (Eds.), *In search of cultural competence in evaluation: Toward principles and practices. New Directions for Evaluation, 102,* 5–19.

Smith, L. T. (1999). *Decolonizing methodologies: Research and indigenous peoples.* London: Zed Books.

KAREN E. KIRKHART is a professor in the School of Social Work, College of Human Ecology, Syracuse University.

Brandon, P. R. (2011). Reflection on four multisite evaluation case studies. In J. A. King &
F. Lawrenz (Eds.), *Multisite evaluation practice: Lessons and reflections from four cases. New
Directions for Evaluation, 129,* 87–95.

9

Reflection on Four Multisite Evaluation Case Studies

Paul R. Brandon

Abstract

*What do the findings of four National Science Foundation evaluation case stud-
ies suggest to an evaluation scholar who was not part of the research team that
created them? This chapter carefully reviews the cases and summarizes their
comparative findings. The four Beyond Use case studies add to the literature on
levels of evaluation use, with the findings suggesting a level of involvement not
surprising for multisite evaluations like these. Other results indicate that the levels of findings use were greater than the levels of stakeholder involvement
reported and that a substantial portion of the use reported in the case studies
was process use. Interpreting the reported relationships between stakeholder
involvement and use must be done cautiously, but it remains true that showing
a causal relationship between stakeholder participation in evaluation activities
and the use of evaluation findings is as difficult in these case studies as it has
been in most of the research on that relationship over the past 30 years. The
chapter raises implications for both practice and research on multisite evaluations.* © Wiley Periodicals Inc., and the American Evaluation Association.

The reports of the Beyond Use (see"Editors' Notes," this issue) case
studies address the topics of stakeholder involvement in evaluation
and evaluation use, both in the context of multisite evaluations. The
discussions of stakeholder involvement and evaluation use in the case

NEW DIRECTIONS FOR EVALUATION, no. 129, Spring 2011 © Wiley Periodicals, Inc., and the American Evaluation
Association. Published online in Wiley Online Library (wileyonlinelibrary.com) • DOI: 10.1002/ev.357

studies are the most recent additions to the wide literature on these two topics, but with the exception of the issue edited by Herrell and Straw (2002), little, if anything, has been published about them in the context of multisite evaluations.

In this chapter, I comment on the case studies' findings about involvement and use. My intent is to address issues that I identified in the reports of the case-study findings, as Lawrenz, King, and Ooms (see their article in this issue) did in their cross-case analysis, but from the perspective of an outsider who has conducted multisite educational program evaluations and research on both stakeholder involvement in evaluations and evaluation use. I attend to the case studies, but comment little on the material presented elsewhere in this issue.

Stakeholder Involvement

Stakeholder Roles in the Four Studies

The four case studies occurred in diverse contexts and had diverse expectations about stakeholder involvement. The stakeholders served by the Math Science Partnership's Research, Evaluation, and Technical Assistance teams (MSP-RETA) were involved as part of project evaluation capacity building. The Advanced Technological Education (ATE) project stakeholders were involved in the evaluations primarily through responding to the program-wide evaluators' instruments and reviewing program-wide evaluation results. The Local Systemic Change (LSC) project stakeholders submitted annual reports and participated in annual principal investigator (PI)/evaluator meetings and in training about conducting classroom observations, with most of the substantive involvement occurring only among projects funded in the program's early years. Finally, the Collaboratives for Excellence in Teacher Preparation (CETP) stakeholders participated in evaluation planning, in instrument development, and in responding to instruments in the program-wide evaluation. The CETP stakeholders' involvement should have been the deepest of any of the four projects; however, about one-third of the CETP projects did not provide data to the multisite evaluators. Indeed, stakeholder participation was not even required for the MSP or CETP evaluations (Lawrenz & Huffman, 2003).

The Levels of Stakeholder Involvement in the Four Studies

The findings about stakeholder involvement were reported with varying metrics (scale means or percentages) for the four case studies, making it difficult to rank the programs on the levels of stakeholder involvement. The Utah State MSP-RETA case study notes that involvement in the program's evaluation-related activities was generally low to moderate. The ATE PIs'

NEW DIRECTIONS FOR EVALUATION • DOI: 10.1002/ev

and evaluators' mean ratings on the 13 questionnaire items about their involvement ranged from 2.1 to 2.7 on 4-point scales, and the percentages of respondents indicating they were not involved at all ranged from 37% to 48%. The LSC PIs' and evaluators' mean response to the questionnaire item about overall involvement in the evaluation was 2.7 on a 4-point scale. Of the CETP respondents, the range reporting involvement in various evaluation activities was 22% to 48%.

It might be concluded that the findings suggest that stakeholder involvement should be characterized as ranging from *very little* for the MSP project to *somewhat* for the remaining three evaluations. I suggest that this conclusion would be an erroneous interpretation made in an absolute sense (that is, in light of the scale anchor points) and that the appropriate conclusion is to characterize the findings *as the level of involvement that is likely for multisite evaluations* of the nature reported here. Given the types of evaluation activities in which the stakeholders participated, it is not surprising that the case study results showed relatively low means on the questionnaire items about involvement. The PIs were not the primary audiences for the evaluations, so the evaluations were not as likely to address issues of immediate interest to the responding stakeholders. The core evaluations might have addressed summative issues of interest to the primary audience (NSF program officers), but were unlikely to have addressed formative, immediate-feedback issues of interest to the project PIs and staff. The project PIs were not likely to have as strong a stake in the national NSF evaluations as they would have had their participation been sought or required in their local project evaluations.

Evaluation Use

Probably no topic in the body of research on evaluation has been the focus of more studies than the use of evaluation. Some of the literature on the topic has addressed the use of evaluation findings to make program decisions, understand evaluation contexts, or generate general knowledge—a type of use known as *findings use*. Recently, studies have increasingly examined the effects of evaluation on stakeholders' evaluation knowledge, skills, or attitudes toward evaluation—a type of use known as *process use*.

The Levels of Evaluation Use in the Four Studies

Findings about *levels* of use are rare in the empirical research on evaluation. Recently a coauthor and I (Brandon & Singh, 2009) examined empirical studies of findings use that had been identified in five major literature reviews conducted between 1981 and 2003 and found only five studies that had reported findings on the levels of use. The four Beyond Use case studies add to the literature on levels of evaluation use.

NEW DIRECTIONS FOR EVALUATION • DOI: 10.1002/ev

Findings use. The results indicate that the levels of findings use were, to the extent they can be compared validly, greater than the levels of stakeholder involvement that were reported in the case studies. The projects served by MSP-RETA (about which only qualitative data were collected) reported several examples of use. The percentages of respondents in the LSC project that reported using evaluation findings "at least a little" were above 70% for most of the items about use and were above 60% for CETP respondents. Of the CETP respondents, about 70% said that the core evaluation increased their knowledge of evaluation of science, technology, engineering, and mathematics (STEM) education, and of their projects, at least to a small extent. For ATE, most of the means of the responses to the survey items about use were 2.6 or 2.7.

Because of the scarcity of findings in the literature on the levels of use, the results reported in this issue are a valuable addition to the literature. Similar to the assessment about interpreting the level of stakeholder involvement, I conclude that the mean ratings reported on the scale items about use should be interpreted as the levels that are likely for multisite evaluations of the type examined in the four case studies. That is, they do not indicate disappointingly low use; they indicate the level of use that reasonably can be expected.

Process use. A substantial portion of the use of evaluation reported in the case studies was process use. Process use was manifested in the case studies as stakeholders' increase in evaluation knowledge and skills in instances when they applied this knowledge and these skills in project evaluations and other evaluation or research endeavors, or in changes in their attitudes toward or beliefs about evaluation. For example, the MSP-RETA case documents that involvement focused primarily on professional development and evaluation consulting assistance. The ATE case suggests that of the

> . . . survey respondents who participated in another evaluation after the ATE program evaluations, over 80% reported using what they learned from planning and implementing the evaluation in another context. Survey results suggested that even the least-used aspect of the evaluation, the data-collection instruments, were used to at least a little extent by over 60% of the respondents. (Toal & Gullickson, this issue)

Similarly, the LSC case detailed that roughly 70% reported having used the LSC program evaluation plan as a model for another evaluation and that 87% reported using the LSC data-collection instruments in other evaluation contexts. The CETP case stated that one positive outcome of involvement in planning the CETP evaluation was that some project PIs and evaluators believed they had learned a lot by participating in a collaborative process to evaluate the disparate projects. Also, about 60% of CETP respondents reported that they had adapted the core-evaluation model or used the core-evaluation data-collection instruments for other evaluations. These findings

NEW DIRECTIONS FOR EVALUATION • DOI: 10.1002/ev

reflect Cousins' conclusion (2003, p. 259) that the effects of participatory evaluation (PE) on evaluation use showed that "process use was by far and away the most evident type of use arising from PE activities."

Given that the responding stakeholders in the case studies were secondary users of the findings, it is not surprising that the major influences of the evaluation were instances of process use. Process use was in most cases the most likely manner in which the influence of the evaluation would be shown; indeed, it was not the primary intent of the multisite evaluators to affect project stakeholders' use of the evaluation results (that is, their findings use), because NSF staff was the primary audience.

The personal factor. The results of considerable research over the years have suggested that the degree of findings use and process use is affected by the *personal factor*:

> The "personal factor" appears to be the most important determinant of what impact as well as the type of impact of a given evaluation. The evaluator could enhance use by engaging and involving users early in the evaluation, ensuring strong communication between the producers and users of evaluations, reporting evaluation findings effectively so users can understand and use them for their purposes, and maintaining credibility with the potential users. (Hofstetter & Alkin, 2003, p. 216)

Consistent with this conclusion, the MSP case-study findings showed that evaluator characteristics, such as responsiveness, helpfulness, and flexibility, were likely to affect use. This finding is to be expected because the MSP-RETA's role was to provide technical assistance. However, this finding was largely absent from the results of the other case studies. These findings tend to be different from the literature about the effects of the personal factor, perhaps because of the difference between the type of evaluations conducted for the multisite projects examined in these cases and the local evaluations examined in previous, single-site studies of use, in which project personnel are more motivated to participate as primary intended users of the evaluation results.

The Relationship Between Involvement and Use

The authors of the case studies and the cross-case summary all reported findings about the relationships between stakeholder involvement and evaluation use. For example, the ATE case concluded that people's perceptions of involvement in the ATE evaluation appeared to be stronger for interviewees who also provided input on question development or who were asked to present at a meeting. The LSC case stated that these findings are consistent with the idea that involvement in LSC evaluation activities is associated with the use of the evaluation in later projects and activities. The CETP case indicated that involvement in CETP planning meetings resulted in project leaders and evaluators feeling more committed to the evaluation process.

NEW DIRECTIONS FOR EVALUATION • DOI: 10.1002/ev

People's participation in the Utah State MSP-RETA evaluation capacity-building activities did appear to prompt evaluation use by project leaders and evaluators; six of those interviewed reported that they had strengthened and deepened their evaluation knowledge base through their involvement in the MSP-RETA activities at Utah State.

Interpreting the reported relationships between stakeholder involvement and use should be done in light of several considerations. First, comparisons with findings about the relationship between stakeholder involvement and evaluation use reported previously in the literature are necessarily tentative. Most previous studies of this relationship occurred in single-site studies (for example, see Cousins, 2003). The stakeholders in single-site studies are motivated to use evaluation findings because the findings directly address their projects or programs, or they find that they learn evaluation processes because of participation in various evaluation stages. In contrast, these four case studies address the *secondary use of the evaluation of multiple sites* or, as Kirkhart (this issue) names it, the *unintended use* of the evaluations. This scenario varies considerably from single-site studies in that the findings use in the multisite studies is about the effects on multiproject programs, which are relevant to individual projects and sites to varying degrees and certainly less relevant than the findings of the individual projects. This is shown in the findings of the ATE and LSC multisite evaluations in which the evaluators found that stakeholders were not enthusiastic about their involvement because they found that the multisite questionnaire items were not sufficiently aligned with individual project objectives.

Similarly, PIs and evaluators are likely to manifest process use less in multisite studies than in single-site studies because the multisite efforts cannot devote a level of effort to evaluation training that is comparable to single-site studies. For example, the MSP projects expressed complaints about the limited resources available to provide them with evaluation technical assistance and training. This is an issue of feasibility—one of the four categories of evaluation standards provided in the Joint Committee's Standards for Educational Evaluation (1994)—which is often overlooked in research on evaluation. King, Ross, Callow-Heusser, Gullickson, Lawrenz, and Weiss (this issue) discussed this issue in their multicase conversation. These distinctions between single-site and multisite studies may be obvious, but I find it is warranted to emphasize them here because they were not discussed in depth elsewhere.

A second consideration that should be kept in mind when interpreting the results about the relationship between use and involvement has to do with the feasibility of addressing contextual differences when conducting multisite studies. Similar to the lack of close alignment between the program-wide evaluation foci and the individual-project foci, as reported by some of the project personnel in the case studies, the diverse nature of the many projects across the duration of the four programs could not be taken into account in the four program-wide studies. Kirkhart addresses this diversity and the difficulties of taking it into account in her discussion of the extent to which personal and organizational cultural differences were considered in the four case studies. The evaluators' ambivalence about addressing cultural issues, as expressed in their multicase discussion, shows the difficulty in dealing with these issues. Indeed, to live up to their contractual obligations, multisite evaluators ultimately must ensure that the purpose, methods, and overall pathways of their evaluations address the concerns of the primary intended users, that is, the funding agency. As one of the multisite evaluators stated in the multisite conversation, multisite evaluators should never relinquish control of decisions, even if they choose to involve people in certain ways to increase ownership.

Third, a causal relationship between stakeholder participation in evaluation activities and the use of evaluation findings is as difficult to show in the four case studies as it has been in most of the research on that relationship over the past 30 years. The design of the four case studies is not ideal for showing causality because the studies are observational and involve no systematic manipulation of variables. The co-occurring stakeholder participation and use of evaluation findings that is reported in the case studies might be evidence of a relationship, but the extent to which the former led to the latter can only be surmised. The foundation for making causal claims is further weakened by the self-report data of the case studies. Interview questions and questionnaire items asking program stakeholders to report their use of evaluation findings are subject to socially desirable responses and self-report bias. Stakeholders who have devoted time and resources to evaluations are naturally likely to report that they have used the findings that the evaluations have produced. This caveat applies, of course, to most studies of stakeholder involvement and of evaluation use.

Finally, the quantitative data lend themselves to calculating correlations that would help substantiate the strength of the qualitative conclusions made in the case-study reports. Correlations between the questionnaire items about stakeholder participation and the items about the use of findings are reported in a recent dissertation (Roseland, 2011). Findings from canonical correlation analysis indicate a moderately strong positive correlation between involvement and use in this study. More specifically, the standardized canonical correlation coefficient for the first function produced by the canonical analysis was .558 (31% overlapping variance); the second was 0.13 (2% overlapping variance).

Summary and Suggestions for Future Research

The Beyond Use case studies are characterized by diversity in (a) program purposes and contexts, (b) expectations about stakeholder involvement, (c) forms of intended use, and (d) the methods of data collection about involvement and use. This diversity complicates making comparisons

NEW DIRECTIONS FOR EVALUATION • DOI: 10.1002/ev

among sites and arriving at broad conclusions about the results of the studies, but several conclusions are warranted.

First, it is inappropriate to compare too closely the findings of the four case studies with the findings elsewhere in the broad evaluation literature. The published literature on evaluation use by and large consists of single-site studies in which on-site program personnel are the primary audiences of the evaluations. The case studies reported here address secondary audiences' use of evaluation findings and the unintended effects of involvement on stakeholders' capacities to understand and conduct evaluations (that is, process use). Secondary users in multisite evaluations are less likely to use evaluation findings or processes than primary users in single-site evaluations.

Second, the average ratings and the percentages reported about stakeholder involvement and evaluation use in the four cases were not high, but these results should not be interpreted in an absolute sense (that is, they should not be evaluated against the maximum possible total of scale points or against 100%). Instead, the findings should be interpreted as reflecting the degrees of involvement and levels of use that can reasonably be expected from multisite evaluations in which stakeholders are secondary audiences who are involved in a variety of ways. The degree of stakeholder involvement found in the studies is reasonable because the primary audiences were the NSF program officers, not the project PIs or other project stakeholders. The level of use of the evaluation findings reported in the four case studies is reasonable because, as secondary users, PIs could not be expected to exhibit considerable evaluation use. PIs and project staff are unlikely to be motivated to use the results of evaluations when they are not the primary evaluation audiences. Furthermore, process use is more likely to occur than findings use because PIs are likely to learn about evaluations when they are involved to any degree. Yet even process use is more likely in single-site studies than in multisite studies, because the degree of involvement is much less in the latter than it is in the former.

Third, the relationship reported between stakeholder involvement and evaluation use is difficult to show in the four case studies—indeed, as it has been in studies of single-site evaluations reported in the research-on-evaluation literature over approximately the past 30 years. The program stakeholders interviewed in the Beyond Use case studies reported that stakeholder involvement affected evaluation findings use and process use, but self-report data, which are the primary form of data collected in studies of stakeholder involvement and of evaluation use, are subject to bias. The correlation analyses reported in a recent study (Roseland, 2011) provide additional needed evidence about the relationship between involvement and use.

The results reported in these case studies provide a valuable contribution to the quite sparse literature on multisite evaluations. Much more can be done, of course, to examine the relationship between involvement and use and the degree to which each is reported in multisite studies. Regression analyses with degree of involvement as a predictor variable and level of use as a criterion variable, with moderator or mediator variables about program context included in the models, would provide a more comprehensive look. However, such analyses would require many sites; may not be feasible without significant funding; and, because of the need for many sites, would probably be limited to widely disseminated, stable programs in which stakeholders are not expected to participate much in evaluations. Furthermore, quantitative analyses would not be fully informative without strong qualitative components to provide information about context. Future research is needed and possible, but the complexities noted in the Beyond Use case studies will continue to complicate our understanding of the relationship and use—a methodological and epistemological scenario that is quite familiar to seasoned program evaluators!

References

Brandon, P. R., & Singh, J. M. (2009). The strength of the methodological warrants for the findings of research on program evaluation use. *American Journal of Evaluation, 30*, 123–157.

Cousins, J. B. (2003). Utilization effects of participatory evaluation. In T. Kellaghan & D. L. Stufflebeam (Eds.), *International handbook of educational evaluation* (pp. 245–266). Dordrecht, The Netherlands: Kluwer.

Herrell, J. M., & Straw, R. B. (Eds.). (2002). Conducting multiple site evaluations in real-world settings. *New Directions for Evaluation, 94*.

Hofstetter, C. H., & Alkin, M. C. (2003). Evaluation use revisited. In T. Kellaghan & D. L. Stufflebeam (Eds.), *International handbook on educational evaluation* (pp. 197–220). Dordrecht, The Netherlands: Kluwer Academic.

Joint Committee on Standards for Educational Evaluation. (1994). *The Program Evaluation Standards*. Thousand Oaks, CA: Sage.

Lawrenz, F., & Huffman, D. (2003). How can multi-site evaluations be participatory? *American Journal of Evaluation, 24*, 471–482.

Roseland, D. L. (2011). *An investigation of the relationship between involvement and use of evaluation in four multi-site evaluations* (Unpublished doctoral dissertation). University of Minnesota, Minneapolis.

PAUL R. BRANDON *is professor of education at Curriculum Research & Development Group, College of Education, University of Hawaii at Manoa in Honolulu.*

Goodyear, L. K. (2011). Building a community of evaluation practice within a multisite program. In J. A. King & F. Lawrenz (Eds.), *Multisite evaluation practice: Lessons and reflections from four cases. New Directions for Evaluation, 129,* 97–105.

10

Building a Community of Evaluation Practice Within a Multisite Program

Leslie K. Goodyear

Abstract

*New and novel uses of evaluation processes and findings are possible when a
community of practice develops as evaluation stakeholders participate in multisite evaluations in multiple ways. Developing such communities takes advantage of what makes multisite evaluations special. This chapter uses the example
of the Innovative Technology Experiences for Students and Teachers Program's
Learning Resource Center, funded by the National Science Foundation, to articulate how the provision of evaluation technical assistance to a large, multisite
program and its funded projects can contribute to evaluation use.* © Wiley Periodicals, Inc., and the American Evaluation Association.

The multiple ways in which evaluation stakeholders can participate in
multisite evaluations open the door to new and novel uses of evaluation processes and findings. With thoughtful planning and a will-
ingness to be flexible and capitalize on stakeholders' ideas and energy,
evaluators can foster communities of evaluation practice, develop collec-
tions of evaluation instruments, encourage dissemination of evaluation findings, and build evaluation capacity within the evaluation stakeholder groups,
all of which may contribute to broader and deeper evaluation use. Doing so
takes advantage of what makes multisite evaluations special. This chapter
uses the example of the Innovative Technology Experiences for Students and

NEW DIRECTIONS FOR EVALUATION, no. 129, Spring 2011 © Wiley Periodicals, Inc., and the American Evaluation
Association. Published online in Wiley Online Library (wileyonlinelibrary.com) • DOI: 10.1002/ev.358

Teachers (ITEST) Program's Learning Resource Center (LRC) to articulate how the provision of evaluation technical assistance to a large, multisite program and its funded projects can contribute to evaluation use.

First, background about the National Science Foundation's (NSF) ITEST program and its Learning Resource Center will set the stage for this discussion. The ITEST program was conceived in 2003 in direct response to concerns and projections about the growing demand for science, technology, engineering, and mathematics (STEM) professionals and information technology workers in the United States. Driven by the need to ensure a high-quality future STEM workforce to meet U.S. technology needs, the NSF created the ITEST program. The LRC, funded in ITEST's first year, was charged with supporting projects in achieving the program's goals. All ITEST projects are required to have a project-level evaluation, and the LRC compiles findings from those evaluations to inform NSF. However, to date, there has been no program-level evaluation of the ITEST program.

Since 2003, the ITEST program has funded eight cohorts of 3-year, renewable projects—more than 161 in all—and these projects are working with teachers and students in 39 states. ITEST projects target students from rural, urban, and suburban geographies and populations underrepresented in STEM careers—girls, students with disabilities, and students of color— engaging them in innovative, hands-on STEM experiences. ITEST grantee organizations include universities, community-based organizations, science museums, and nonprofit organizations.

The ITEST LRC assists projects through a menu of services that includes technical assistance (TA), networking, opportunities for collaboration, and coordination of dissemination. As originally conceived, the ITEST LRC has four goals: to facilitate collaboration between funded projects; to tighten the research–practice cycle through bringing relevant research to the ITEST projects and encouraging them to contribute to the knowledge base; to compile and disseminate ITEST project models, materials, practices, resources, and publications; and to provide technical assistance to projects on topics that range from strategies for recruiting and retaining teachers and students to writing annual reports to NSF, working with specific technologies, and strategies for disseminating findings. TA takes the form of in-person meetings and workshops at the annual PI Summit, topical conference calls over the course of a year, Web casts and on-line discussions, and responses to individual concerns and issues.

Early in its first year, the LRC staff realized that ITEST projects had a great deal of expertise to offer each other regarding important topics such as project-based learning, the recruitment of participants, STEM content, and so on. This realization confirmed the importance of a collaborative approach to providing technical assistance to the projects. However, during the first year of the program, as project staff began requesting assistance with evaluation from the ITEST LRC, the LRC staff also realized that the evaluation capacity of projects was more varied than expected. This realization provided the impetus to develop a framework and TA activities targeted at increasing the projects' evaluation capacity.

These realizations and demand for evaluation assistance informed the development of the LRC's evaluation technical assistance framework. Embedded within the larger ITEST technical assistance plan, the evaluation TA approach focused on two things: (a) developing an evaluation community of practice that could serve as peer support for evaluators and principal investigators (PIs), and (b) providing relevant, responsive evaluation technical assistance in the form of events, meetings, discussion groups, dissemination opportunities, and products that would both support and be supported by the developing community of practice.

Three assumptions framed the LRC's evaluation technical assistance:

1. Projects have expertise to share with each other, and, at every opportunity, this expertise should be promoted and highlighted. For example, when a project PI or evaluator calls for evaluation TA, in addition to offering advice and pointing the caller to resources or experts in the field, the LRC makes it a point to connect the caller to at least one or two other ITEST project PIs or evaluators who may have advice or expertise to offer. Not only does this leverage the larger ITEST community's expertise for its members' benefit, it develops the understanding that participants in the ITEST program form a community or professional network.

2. Evaluation technical assistance—even very methodologically oriented technical assistance—should include all ITEST community members, not just evaluators. This is important to the LRC for two reasons. First, for evaluators and PIs to work closely together in their evaluative work, PIs need to feel included in evaluation conversations. There are many opportunities for evaluators and PIs to misunderstand each other or for PIs to feel threatened by evaluators; evaluation technical assistance should not contribute to those misunderstandings. Second, the LRC has found that the more PIs understand about evaluation, the more they will support their project evaluations and use evaluation findings. Over time, skeptical PIs have seemed to come around to understanding the value of evaluation through participation in the LRC's TA events and the activities that were organized for PIs and evaluators to work together. In addition, the LRC reminds evaluators that the better their working relationship with PIs, the better the chance their evaluations will get used. For example, a PI who was skeptical of the value of the ITEST LRC—and in particular the value of evaluation—learned how to work more closely with her evaluator to collect useful data. As a result, she served as a featured project on a TA conference call that highlighted innovative dissemination strategies.

NEW DIRECTIONS FOR EVALUATION • DOI: 10.1002/ev

3. The evaluation community of practice belongs to the ITEST community, not to the LRC. The staff at the LRC serve as facilitators of the community through evaluation TA offerings and coordination of community events. However, the community is only as strong as its members' participation. This value is enforced through purposeful responsiveness to ideas the ITEST evaluation community members pose—acting on suggestions to develop products like the On-Line Instrument Database (described later in this chapter) or bringing small groups of community members together to discuss pressing evaluation issues facing their projects. The LRC also reminds community members that they are the arbiters of quality within their community; they should bring the high standards they use in their own work to the activities and work of the community.

The LRC's evaluation technical assistance has four major goals:

1. Support the ITEST project evaluators in doing their work by providing resources, products, and connections with experts.
2. Help project PIs better understand the project evaluation processes and products so that they can work effectively with their evaluators and use the project evaluation's findings.
3. Develop a strong network of evaluators across the ITEST program, all working on similar projects, who can serve as support to each other.
4. Share the evaluation learning and evaluation findings with the ITEST and broader evaluation communities, including staff at the National Science Foundation.

Although these goals are articulated as separate, they are interconnected; actual TA activities and services often incorporate multiple goals. In addition, community building, technical assistance, and dissemination build off of each other. For example, TA helps build community by connecting projects to each other, a community of practice ensures dissemination, and active dissemination creates information for use in TA. These goals build on the articulated TA assumptions and are embodied in the evaluation technical assistance offerings of the ITEST LRC. What follows is a description of the evaluation TA activities offered by the LRC and its connection to evaluation capacity building and evaluation use.

Just-in-Time Individual Project Evaluation Technical Assistance

This includes answering questions about evaluation management, expectations, and in some cases conducting "evaluation marriage counseling." Project evaluators or PIs can call the ITEST LRC and talk with an evaluation TA liaison about their evaluation issues and challenges, whether they be methodological or relational. Depending on the issues presented, the TA liaison will engage in discussion about resources (print, electronic, or expert), suggest that the PI or evaluator contact staff at another ITEST project that has experienced similar issues and may have advice, or offer to help mediate between the PI and the evaluator to troubleshoot the issues. As mentioned before, many ITEST PIs have not worked closely with evaluators before, and there are times that PIs and evaluators have different expectations for the evaluation process and product. The ITEST LRC can serve as a neutral party in these situations to assist the PI and evaluator in working out a plan of action to solve emerging problems. Again, learnings from the evaluation TA work of the ITEST LRC suggest that increased understanding of evaluation on the part of PIs and project staff encourages evaluation use.

An Annual "Evaluation Peer Exchange"

The evaluation peer exchange is a moderated electronic list-serv on which evaluators and project PIs can talk amongst themselves, asking questions, sharing information, and troubleshooting common issues in evaluation. This on-line discussion list offers ITEST community members the chance to learn who among them has expertise in certain evaluation methods or approaches and who might be experiencing the same challenges or issues related to evaluation. For example, project PIs and evaluators post questions about challenges related to measuring certain constructs, such as STEM career interest. A project evaluator might be looking for a validated instrument or just measurement from those who are working with similar projects. In addition, the ITEST LRC evaluation staff poses questions to the community to spark discussion; these questions are usually prompted by the issues that have arisen in the individual TA conversations. For instance, the LRC might pose a question about strategies for dealing with Institutional Review Boards (a relevant topic for all ITEST projects), or a question about whether projects are having issues with access to school-district data. In addition to offering ITEST evaluators a forum to talk about their evaluation challenges and questions, the discussion list offers project PIs the opportunity to gain a broader understanding of evaluation beyond the confines of their own project evaluation.

Conference Calls and Web-cast "Live" Technical Assistance Events

These events target any and all evaluators, PIs, and program staff in the ITEST community. They usually occur quarterly and take the form of a conference call with Web-based PowerPoint presentations. Project evaluators and PIs usually serve as panelists, sharing their successes and innovations, oftentimes along with a notable expert on a specific evaluation topic or a knowledgeable NSF program officer. Topics have included cultural competence in evaluation, using evaluation findings, measurement issues in ITEST projects, and evaluators and PIs working together. These events are a more targeted form of TA, meant to share learning and disseminate innovation with the program. In the case of the evaluation-use conference call, for example, projects have presented ways in which they used evaluation findings for program improvement, in demonstrating the value of their project to local audiences, and for broader dissemination of their work through publication.

An Annual Conference Call to Help Projects Understand the NSF Reporting Requirements and How Evaluation Findings Can Support Their Annual Reports

This is a special event in the form of the TA events mentioned above. Hosted in partnership with the lead NSF ITEST program officers, this session outlines the reporting requirements of NSF and tips for incorporating evaluation findings into annual reports. Of all the TA activities the ITEST LRC sponsors, this is the event that most specifically encourages evaluation use. Three projects usually present their approaches to writing their annual reports and talk about how they work with their evaluators to shape the report so that it can present the evaluation findings. The LRC developed this session in response to a suggestion from a PI in the first cohort who wanted guidance both in reporting to NSF and in working with his evaluator. Discussion on these calls often moves from the specifics of writing annual reports to other ways in which project staff can use evaluation findings such as for promoting the project, in grant writing, in recruiting teachers and students to the project, or through publications.

The Annual ITEST PI Meeting

This offers opportunities to present evaluation findings and discuss evaluation issues and challenges. The ITEST LRC hosts an annual PI meeting every February, and for the program's first few years, projects were required to bring their evaluators to these meetings. The main goal was to help the evaluators understand the larger picture of the ITEST program while also offering them the opportunity to meet and network with other evaluators in the same way that project PIs use these meetings to network with other project PIs. A secondary goal was to ensure that evaluation would be a topic on the annual meeting agenda and that project staff would be encouraged to talk about their evaluation work there. Several evaluation-related activities included (a) support-group–like discussions for evaluators to talk about how things were going and get feedback and support from other evaluators (LRC staff used this as an opportunity to track what kinds of issues evaluators were facing and think about how these issues could be addressed in the coming year's evaluation technical assistance program), (b) presentations from NSF personnel about their vision for evaluation at the project level, and (c) presentations made by project evaluator/PI pairs in which they discussed the previous year's evaluation findings and what actions they were taking as a result. These activities were meant both to highlight evaluation within the ITEST community and to encourage evaluators and PIs to work closely together to use evaluation findings for project improvement. Evaluators who attended reportedly left with a new sense of the larger scope of the ITEST program and with innovative ideas gathered from networking with other project evaluators. With regard to evaluation, project PIs appeared to gain a sense of the possibilities for using evaluation processes and products to inform project decision making and to demonstrate their project's value.

Opportunity to Join One or More Research Working Groups to Explore Cross-Project Research on Specific STEM or Evaluation Issues

During the first year of the program, the ITEST LRC developed the working-group concept to advance a cross-project research agenda. The ITEST LRC adapted the participatory multisite model Lawrenz and Huffman (2003) articulated, and encouraged PIs and evaluators to participate in multiple brainstorming sessions developing themes for working groups and research topics that would be investigated. One of these working-group topics was called "embedded evaluation"—evaluation activities embedded in project activities. A group of mostly evaluators and some PIs met to discuss the ways in which they had embedded evaluation activities into project activities, such as, for example, games that served as performance measures for skill development or content knowledge. This group decided that it would be a contribution to the community (a) to articulate a common definition of what constituted embedded evaluation, (b) to develop a template for documenting an embedded evaluation process or procedure, and (c) to compile these templates in a searchable archive that would be accessible to other ITEST projects. Members of the group exchanged ideas and techniques for embedding evaluation activities and later presented together at the ITEST PI meeting, then again at the American Evaluation Association (AEA) conference.

The Development of an On-Line, Searchable Evaluation Instrument Database

LRC staff encouraged projects to submit their instruments for inclusion in an on-line instrument database, which is housed within the ITEST On-Line Community Web site. Instruments the LRC receives are coded for type of instrument and content covered so that the database is searchable on common keywords used to code the instruments. Although the instruments in this database are not vetted for quality, nor are they required to include reliability data, there is a set of rules and understandings that guide fair use of the instruments in the database; both those submitting and using the instruments are bound by these rules. The instrument database is only for use by those within the ITEST community. In the database currently are interview guides, focus-group guides, observation guides, and survey instruments, totaling about 100 instruments. Access to this database increases evaluation resources available to the professional learning communities, a visible form of capacity building.

Coordination of Conference and Publication Opportunities

The ITEST LRC staff actively seeks out opportunities for project participants to disseminate their work at national forums, including conferences such as the American Evaluation Association, the American Educational Research Association, the Society for Information Technology and Teacher Education, and the National Science Teachers Association, and in publications such as the *Journal of Technology* and *Teacher Education* (for example, Goodyear & Carlson, 2007). The ITEST LRC coordinates with interested project PIs and evaluators to form panels and submit conference proposals. By doing this, project staff are able to present to new audiences at national conferences and to leverage publication opportunities that may not have been available to them individually. With regard to the projects' evaluation work, ITEST evaluators have presented numerous times at the AEA conference. The ITEST LRC staff has, in addition to coordinating those conference presentations, hosted meetings at these conferences for the evaluators to talk and network.

All of these technical assistance offerings are meant to contribute to the development of a community of evaluation practice within the ITEST program community. This interactive network among the project PIs and evaluators— the community of practice—contributes to evaluation use by building evaluation capacity; evaluators' capacity is increased through learning new techniques and ideas from peers, and PIs' evaluation capacity develops as they learn more about evaluation generally and are exposed to the multiple possible uses for evaluation processes and findings. The ITEST LRC has taken what might be considered a challenging evaluation context—the multisite ITEST program—and leveraged it to develop these activities and the community of evaluation practice. The diversity of interests, approaches, and outcomes within the ITEST program sets the stage for a dynamic, multifaceted network of evaluators and PIs to collaborate with one another to create something that is more than the sum of its parts.

Conclusions

Obviously, there have been challenges along the way. The community of practice for ITEST evaluation is diverse and has varied levels of need and expertise; in spite of their apparent need for assistance, not all ITEST evaluators or PIs have participated in the evaluation TA offerings. Evaluation technical assistance is but one small part of the scope of the ITEST LRC, and, although it is important, time and resources have not always allowed it to be as robust as it could have been. However, these challenges have not stood in the way of achieving some successes with regard to promoting evaluation capacity, peer-to-peer learning, and evaluation use. As a result of the ITEST LRC's evaluation technical assistance, a lively, active evaluation community of practice has blossomed within the ITEST program. Over the 5 years, there were roughly 150 posts to the evaluation peer exchange, which is just one activity. Most project evaluators and PIs participated at least once, and about a third of them participated regularly. Evaluation processes and findings have been shared in multiple venues—project-to-project through the on-line discussions and conference calls, to the NSF and other project audiences at the PI meetings, and more broadly to new audiences at conferences and through publications. In addition, new conversations about evaluation have been sparked at the project, LRC, NSF, and field levels, and, according to project PIs and NSF program officers, evaluation is informing both project and program decision making.

The LRC has documented ways in which the ITEST evaluation community of practice has contributed to evaluation capacity building among the ITEST projects. However, research could be conducted to understand the specific benefits to PIs and evaluators of participation in such a community and the multiple and complex ways such participation fosters evaluation use. In addition, more research could help us understand the ultimate contribution of such evaluation capacity building among projects and their evaluators to program-level evaluation.

References

Goodyear, L., & Carlson, B. (2007). The ITEST Learning Resource Center's online evaluation database: Examples from the collection. *International Journal of Technology in Teaching and Learning, 3*(1), 51–65.

Lawrenz, F., & Huffman, D. (2003). How can multi-site evaluations be participatory? *American Journal of Evaluation, 24*(4), 471–482.

LESLIE K. GOODYEAR *is a senior research scientist at Education Development Center in Newton, Massachusetts. Program evaluation was the focus of her doctoral work in Human Service Studies at Cornell University.*

Mark, M. M. (2011). Toward better research on—and thinking about—evaluation influence, especially in multisite evaluations. In J. A. King & F. Lawrenz (Eds.), *Multisite evaluation practice: Lessons and reflections from four cases. New Directions for Evaluation, 129,* 107–119.

11

Toward Better Research On—and Thinking About—Evaluation Influence, Especially in Multisite Evaluations

Melvin M. Mark

Abstract

Evaluation is typically carried out with the intention of making a difference in the understandings and actions of stakeholders and decision makers. The author provides a general review of the concepts of evaluation "use," evaluation "influence," and "influence pathways," with connections to multisite evaluations. The study of evaluation influence and influence pathways is briefly discussed.© Wiley Periodicals, Inc., and the American Evaluation Association.

The practice of evaluation is generally undertaken not as an esoteric academic enterprise, but as an activity that can make a difference. Evaluators from different traditions disagree, sometimes vigorously, about what particular kind of difference they hope to make. Indeed, what may appear to be debates about methods often are debates about the kind of consequences that different evaluators want their work to have (Mark,

The author gratefully acknowledges the assistance of Kelli Johnson, Denise Roseland, and Stacie Toal. These three research assistants on the "Beyond Use" project expertly and graciously contributed examples from the multisite evaluations examined in that project.

2009). Regardless, most (if not all) evaluators share the general idea that evaluation should have consequences—consequences that go beyond the journal citations, peer regard, and grants that appear to suffice for basic researchers.

The literature on evaluation use arose in part because aspirations about evaluation's consequences during the field's rapid expansion in the 1960s and 1970s were not widely met. Early evaluators observed that their evaluations did not routinely appear to change the decisions that were made (or not made) about programs and policies. This seeming shortage of use then helped stimulate research on use from the mid-1970s to early 1980s. Research findings from that time continue to shape thinking about evaluation use today. For example, research from that period showing the importance of a champion of evaluation within an agency (Patton et al., 1977) still underlies the central rationale for the popular utilization-focused evaluation model (Patton, 2008). As another example, research from the 1970s (for example, Weiss & Bucavalas, 1977) informs the still widely recognized notion of conceptual use or enlightenment. Indeed, until the past decade it was easy to find taxonomies of evaluation use that relied solely on findings and ideas developed by the early 1980s. More recently, however, later empirical and conceptual work has helped expand earlier views of evaluation use (Patton, 2008).

The current chapter aspires to add to a continuing conversation about the consequences of evaluation. In this chapter, I offer a set of general observations, setting the stage with a selective review of ideas about evaluation use, followed by a brief summary of the concepts of evaluation influence and influence pathways. Then I very briefly sketch out alternatives for studying evaluation influence, address in general terms some possible objections, and point toward next steps. This chapter also aspires to contribute in part to the theory and practice of multisite evaluations. Accordingly, I address issues of evaluation use and influence in the context of multisite evaluations.

Standard Views About Use

There is no shortage of summaries of the history of past thinking about evaluation use and related concepts (for example, Leviton & Hughes, 1981; Nutley, Walter, & Davies, 2007). As is widely noted, different forms or types of use exist. Although there is general agreement that different types of use exist, the types listed may vary across publications. Still, a degree of consensus exists. In particular, most presentations of evaluation use distinguish between (a) direct or instrumental use (that is, direct action, such as voting for a policy or modifying a program) and (b) conceptual use or enlightenment (that is, changed or new understandings or ways of thinking). Examples come from the "Beyond Evaluation Use" (see "Editors' Notes," this issue) case evaluations:

- As a multisite setting, the Advanced Technological Education (ATE) program illustrates direct evaluation use, particularly related to the annual Web-based survey component of its program evaluation. ATE project leaders reported using the survey results to make decisions about how to move ahead, for instance.
- ATE project leaders also reported using survey results to broaden their perspective beyond the local project level, an example of conceptual use.
- The Collaboratives for Excellence in Teacher Preparation (CETP) evaluation also provides examples of instrumental use. In that multisite program evaluation, local project leaders were invited to collaborate with the core program evaluator to develop instruments and protocols for data collection. Some CETP project leaders reported frequently referencing the CETP protocols, modifying them for use in other projects.
- In the multisite Local Systemic Change (LSC) program, a local project leader reported that the evaluation led him to recognize that classroom inquiry without concern for the quality of that activity—"activity for activity's sake"—was something to be avoided. The evaluation changed his understanding of how classroom activities should be constructed—conceptual use.

Perhaps the third most frequently listed category in taxonomies of use is so-called political or symbolic use (although these are sometimes differentiated). Typically, the image portrayed is of a politician who spouts evaluation findings if (and only if) the findings suit his or her prior preferences. Or of evaluation being called for as a tactic to delay widespread action. Political use was originally, and to an extent still is, portrayed as inappropriate. However, an alternative view holds that political use is neither surprising nor a cause for criticism (Leviton & Hughes, 1981). Perhaps we should be pleased, rather than critical, if quality evaluation findings are brought to the debate and deliberation by a partisan politician whose preexisting position is supported.

Taxonomies of use increasingly include two additional categories. First, process use refers to consequences that arise not because of evaluation findings, but rather because of people's involvement in the process of an evaluation. For example, evaluation planning might lead program staff to have more of a shared vision of the program and its purposes. The Utah State Math and Science Partnership: Research, Evaluation, and Technical Assistance (MSP-RETA) program provides an example. Many MSP project leaders remarked that the act of engaging in evaluation planning allowed the project team early on to think about a common vision and desired outcomes. The "Beyond Evaluation Use" survey provides additional reports of process use. A majority of respondents from the ATE, CETP, and LSC program evaluations reported that participation in the program evaluation increased their knowledge and skills about evaluation. Among CETP survey respondents who had subsequently conducted another evaluation, approximately 60% reported using the CETP program evaluation as a model, and two-thirds stated they had used data-collection instruments developed for the CETP core evaluation in another evaluation. Respondents from the LSC program evaluation showed comparable and even stronger findings.

Taxonomies of use today also may include what Weiss and her colleagues have described as imposed use (Weiss, Murphy-Graham, & Birkeland, 2005). Imposed use occurs when people are mandated to use the results of evaluation, or at least believe they are so mandated. For example, substance-abuse programs may be on an "approved list" by virtue of favorable findings from an evaluation that passes specified screening criteria, and school administrators may believe they are required to select a program from that list in order to receive federal funding. The ATE evaluation provides what appears to be an alternative form of mandated use. As part of that multisite evaluation, the evaluation team developed a Web-based annual survey. After the overarching program evaluation had ended, National Science Foundation (NSF) officials still insisted that local projects complete the annual survey, a use that was mandated. (As this example illustrates, mandated use can overlap with other categories, notably instrumental use.)

In a sense, it is relatively simple to apply ideas of use to multisite evaluations. As the preceding examples suggest, any type of use can arise from a multisite evaluation. In another sense, multisite evaluations bring a certain complexity (in the old sense of the term). To take but one complicating factor, in a multisite evaluation use can take place in at least two kinds of locations, central and local. First, central decision makers can make use of evaluation findings, as when NSF program officers change the program announcement for a next round of funding competition or a member of Congress cites evaluation findings when arguing for continued appropriations. Process use is also possible, as when a program officer comes to think differently about a program because of his or her participation in evaluation planning. Second, local use can occur, for example, when the director of the Philadelphia site adjusts program operations based on an evaluation finding. Moreover, cases of local use can vary in terms of how widespread they are. A particular form of local use may occur at only one of many sites, or may occur at all sites (without central involvement), or may occur at a portion of the sites. As I briefly discuss later, the pattern of local use may be of interest and potentially revealing for understanding evaluation's consequences.

Shortcomings of Use

Although valuable in many ways, taxonomies of types of use—such as instrumental, conceptual, political, process, and imposed use—are not without their shortcomings. First, there is a bit of an apples–oranges–tofu problem. Imagine that a third-party observer, armed with observations, interviews, surveys and more, has constructed the story of how some form of use has occurred as a result of an evaluation. Perhaps, for example, an NSF program officer read an evaluation report, thought about the implications of a key finding, and persuaded senior NSF leadership of the finding's importance; imagine further that the senior NSF leaders then met with key Congressional staffers, who inserted language in an appropriation bill that subsequently was passed after the evaluation findings were cited during Congressional debate.

Instrumental and conceptual use both refer to what might be considered "end-state" uses. These types of use tell something about the end of the story about evaluation's consequences. For example, the story may end with legislators voting in favor of the program because of the evaluation findings (instrumental) or with people having a different understanding of the nature of the problem or the range of potential solutions (conceptual). Similarly, the concept of political use often (but not inevitably) refers to the end of the story, with a politician brandishing evaluation findings in support of his or her preferred position. However, the idea of political use focuses on the actor's role (for example, a politician) and motivation (for example, to support a preexisting position), more so than on the nature of the use itself (which could also be labeled a kind of direct use).

The notion of process use, in contrast, usually tells us something about the beginning of the story, not the end. It tells us that the story of evaluation's consequences started because of people's involvement in the evaluation process. But the end of the story might be either instrumental or conceptual (or perhaps something else). Imposed use tells us more, including something about the middle of the story of the evaluation's consequences (the program is included on an approved list) and something about the end-state use (for example, adoption by a school district).

In short, the standard types of use focus on different aspects of the story of an evaluation's consequences. For some purposes, it would be valuable to have a framework that attends to the initial inputs of evaluation's consequences, on through to the ultimate outcomes of interest that arise from evaluation, with attention also to key steps in the middle. This notion is addressed further momentarily in terms of influence pathways. In addition, someone who loves conceptually clean classification systems could argue simply that the apples–oranges–tofu nature of the list of types of use suggests the need for an alternative formulation.

Another characteristic of use as a concept is that, at least in many formulations, it is restricted to local effects of evaluation, that is, to changes that are close in time and place to the evaluation (Hofstetter & Alkin, 2003). In addition, the term can imply a kind of intentionality and awareness, with the users of evaluation knowing that they are using it. But evaluation can have important consequences that are removed from the location of the evaluation. Indeed, a key way that state-level evaluations matter is that they can affect decisions made in other states. For instance, legislators in New York may be influenced, directly or indirectly, by the results of an evaluation from Texas. Though not specifically related to legislative activity, the MSP-RETA program provides an example of nonlocal effects of evaluation influence. The MSP-RETA created a network of evaluation experts to provide on-demand technical assistance to MSP grantees. The number of such requests was lower than anticipated, and so the direct influence of the MSP-RETA was thought to be quite small. However, another product of the MSP-RETA project was the development of the design–implementation–outcomes (DIO) model, which has been much more widely used across the wide range of MSP projects. In addition, although not cited in the formal literature, many references to this model occur on the NSF Web site and in papers and presentations in the gray literature. Thus, influence occurred beyond the confines of the original target audience for the MSP-RETA project. In addition, evaluation sometimes makes a difference even though the parties involved are unaware of the evaluation or at least of its effects on them. For example, legislation may be passed that is affected by previous evaluation, even if the legislators who vote on it are unaware of how or when the evaluation results made a difference while the legislation was drafted. To illustrate, eventually some users of the DIO model may be unaware of its origin in MSP-RETA.

Consider the preceding limitations of the concept of use as applied to multisite evaluations. For some purposes, it would be valuable to know the beginning, middle, and end of the story of how evaluation came to make a difference in multisite evaluations. For instance, imagine that a key form of instrumental use occurred, with most or all sites revising their program activities in a way suggested by evaluation findings. Implication for future evaluations and for conceptualizations about evaluation's consequences would seem to differ, depending on whether the change was imposed centrally (but not implemented in all cases) or instead was adopted initially by a notable site and diffused across sites because of the persuasive power of that site's director. More generally, knowing *why* some form of use occurred, not only *that* it occurred, can be informative.

As an example, in CETP the program evaluator met with mature CETPs (those that had at least 3 years of funding and their own local evaluations already completed) and gathered instruments from the local projects, as well as from other respected sources in science, technology, engineering, and mathematics (STEM) education. CETP project staffs were invited to critique the instruments and to contribute to the development of new, shared instruments that would be used to collect program-level data in the newly funded multisite program evaluation. Next, the CETP program evaluator convened a meeting of CETP projects with fewer than 3 years of funding. Feedback from meeting participants showed their enthusiasm about the instruments and their intent to use them in local project evaluations. The NSF program officer for CETP believed that the projects felt a greater sense of ownership over the core data because of their involvement in creation of the instruments and protocols and therefore were more likely to use the data. In addition, the program officer believed that the larger multisite program evaluation instruments made the projects gather higher-level data about their project's impact. Understanding why use occurred is itself a form of learning that can contribute to subsequent action.

In addition, at least sometimes in multisite evaluations, an implicit (if not explicit) objective is to influence future actions at other locations (where, say, services are offered but not under the funding stream associated with the evaluation). In simple terms, the idea is that evaluation will contribute to more widespread dissemination and adoption of effective practices beyond the scope of the evaluation. In at least some cases, as change diffuses, the role of evaluation in the process will become invisible to those who are adopting it. For example, knowledge of the evaluation may affect early adopters, but later adopters may be influenced by the early adopters but not know of the evaluation. This pattern clearly falls under the broader umbrella of influence, but may not fall under more restrictive definitions of use.

Influence and Influence Pathways

In 2000, Karen Kirkhart argued for a focus on evaluation influence rather than use. Evaluation influence explicitly includes both changes that take place at the location and general time frame of the evaluation and changes that take place elsewhere and later. Influence also accommodates those cases in which change takes place because of an evaluation, but individuals involved are unaware of the role of evaluation in that change. Kirkhart (2000) offered an "integrated theory" that conceptualizes evaluation influence in three dimensions: source (evaluation findings versus evaluation process), intention (for example, intended use versus unintended effects of evaluation), and time (essentially, short, interim, and long term). Henry and Mark (2003a), Mark and Henry (2004), and Mark (2006) strove to add to the conception of influence. Part of this work involved an effort to identify and categorize several different mechanisms or processes that might be involved in the longer storyline of evaluation's consequences—an endeavor that is important but potentially more challenging in the context of multisite evaluations.

The basic ideas are simple. First and foremost, in thinking about evaluation use and influence, something like a logic model or program theory should be helpful. In essence, this would involve laying out the multiple steps by which evaluation findings or process eventually leads (or fails to lead) to downstream consequences of interest. Thinking like a program-theory–driven evaluator, what is the sequence of processes by which an evaluation comes to have its effects (if any)? Mark and Henry call models of the steps through which evaluation may make a difference "influence pathways" and suggest such models may have several benefits.

One potential benefit could arise when an influence pathway is developed as an upfront, developmental activity. That is, thinking in advance about how the evaluation may come to make a difference could affect evaluation planning (for example, suggesting the need for a more varied reporting and communication plan; recognizing that an additional outcome needs to be measured to persuade a key evaluation audience). This idea is similar to the widespread observation that the process of developing a program theory sometimes leads to program modification. Given the possible emergent nature of opportunities for influence, however, an evaluation pathway for planning probably should be revisited and revised periodically. An example of the benefits of thinking about influence pathways comes from the ATE program evaluation. The evaluators devoted considerable time and energy to their dissemination strategy, which evolved over the 7 years of the evaluation. In addition to revising the dissemination methods, the program evaluators also reported that their interactions with NSF personnel as part of their dissemination activity led them to make changes in the evaluation itself. Specifically, they modified survey items so they could better meet NSF's identified information needs (Lawrenz, Gullickson, & Toal, 2007).

Henry and Mark (2003b), Mark and Henry (2004), and Mark (2006) also offered an evolving list of different kinds of processes that might be involved in the influence pathways emanating from various evaluations. Their idea was that for evaluators and others who try to construct or study evaluation pathways, it could be useful to have a listing to draw on of processes that might be operating. By way of analogy, it is as though these authors had tried to lay out the different general theories of change that could underlie programs, but their focus instead was on possible interim processes and outcomes for the theories of change from evaluation itself as an intervention in the world. Unfortunately, the message may have been lost that the full list of processes and outcomes is not intended to be included or studied in every evaluation pathway. Rather, the full list is meant as a kind of conceptual menu or generic model, available to help guide the construction of specific evaluation pathways for particular evaluations or particular studies of evaluation influence.

I will not attempt to repeat that entire menu here and will instead simply sketch its structure. The model posits that the processes evaluation helps stimulate (and the eventual evaluation consequences we may be interested in) can operate at different *levels of analysis*. Although the lines could be drawn differently, the model identifies changes at three levels: the individual, the interpersonal, and the collective. In addition to the three levels of analysis, the model specifies different *kinds of consequences* that evaluation can have. These include both cognitive/affective and behavioral consequences. These two categories correspond to conceptual and direct (instrumental) use, respectively. However, Mark and Henry did not employ these more familiar terms, because, for example, certain kinds of behavior may occur as shorter-term processes that lead to a downstream form of influence. That is, cognitive/affective and behavioral effects can appear at the end of the story of evaluation's consequences, or earlier on, or both.

Mark and Henry (2004) also describe two other types of consequences: general influence processes (such as "elaboration," or thinking at some depth about evaluation findings or processes) and motivational processes (such as increasing program staff efforts via standard setting). These two categories are likely to be of interest only in the middle of the story of evaluation's consequences. That is, they are primarily of interest as interim processes that may lead to a downstream consequence of interest. Mark (2006) added another category of evaluation consequences, tentatively labeled as "relational consequences." This category includes changes resulting from evaluation, not in behavior or attitude, but in aspects of ongoing relationships, structures, and organizational processes (for example, creation of a democratic forum for deliberation [House & Howe, 1999] or the development of a learning organization [Preskill & Torres, 1998]).

In addition to the general categories of evaluation consequences, Mark and Henry identify specific processes that correspond to each category at the individual, interpersonal, and collective levels. As this brief sketch suggests, the result is complex. However, as noted previously, it is intended as a kind of meta-model, guiding the construction of specific evaluation pathways for a given evaluation. In particular, one can draw on the model—or on information from other literatures or background knowledge, or both—to build influence pathways for evaluations, analogous to program theories for programs. These can be employed a priori, before the evaluation takes place. Or they may be built early on and then revised periodically to capture changes from learning and revisions due to new opportunities. Or they may be reconstructed descriptively after the fact to study what the consequences of evaluation were and why. As an aside, a single a priori influence model is unlikely to suffice because we do not know the evaluation's findings in advance. In this sense, the analogy to program theory fits better for emergent programs that will be developed by a partnership, rather than a program that is defined in detail in advance.

Thinking about multisite evaluations highlights that, in most cases, multiple influence pathways are possible. In the case of multisite evaluations, evaluation influence may operate from central to local levels (as in the case of imposed use), from site to site and beyond (as in the case of diffusion), from local site to the central level (as when project directors use evaluation finding to lobby central decision makers for a change), and in more complicated versions with three or more steps and perhaps other actors outside of the multisite evaluation context. Through its development over time, the CETP program evaluation illustrates several different influence pathways. Initially, NSF required each CETP project to conduct its own project-level evaluation. As these project evaluations progressed, however, the evaluators came together across sites—an example of diffusion of influence—and agreed upon ways to enhance the overall CETP evaluation by increasing collaboration among evaluators.

Several years later, building upon the recommendations from two meetings of the CETP project principal investigators (PIs), NSF funded a national, overarching program-level evaluation effort, an example of influence from local sites to the central level. Although NSF encouraged all

19 CETP projects funded from 1993 to 2000 to participate in the national impact evaluation, participation in the evaluation was voluntary, and in the end only 12 of the 19 CETPs actually provided usable data. Different CETPs also provided different types of data, so the numbers of projects providing any one type of data varied. In turn, it is not difficult to understand why the CETP case showed only a modest relationship between project involvement in the CETP evaluation and influence of the evaluation's processes and products on the projects. Some projects were already past the formative stages, and they were not able to use the data from the multisite program evaluation, indicating that central to local influence may vary from one local site to another. As the CETP example suggests, multiple pathways may exist for the different consequences of evaluation. For instance, the steps involved in getting to modifications of the program at an existing site may be quite different from the steps involved in getting to funding for additional sites, even when the same evaluation contributed to both.

The most reasonable position may be to see use and influence not as competing concepts, but as complementary ones available to inform the planning, conduct, and study of evaluation. That is, broadening focus from evaluation use to evaluation influence does not necessarily diminish the importance of classic forms of use or of intended use by intended users. Rather, the broader scope can perhaps encourage us to think about a wider range of the ways evaluation makes a difference. In evaluation practice, evaluators can strive to maximize the likelihood both of (intended) use and emerging opportunities for influence. In research on evaluation, the researcher can choose to examine use more narrowly defined, influence more broadly defined, or both.

Studying Evaluation Influence

In this section, I briefly offer selected, tentative suggestions for research on evaluation influence. First, a wide array of methods is available for the study of evaluation influence, just as a wide range of methods is available for evaluating programs and policies or for studying any other social process. Lawrenz, King, and Ooms (this issue) give a more specific answer in their discussion of the implications of multisite evaluation for research, focusing on four methods they see as especially salient for the study of influence. Second, the existence and quality of the relevant theory of change, in the form of an influence pathway, should affect the selection of methods for studying evaluation influence. For instance, with a well-founded influence pathway in hand, relatively fixed methods (for example, a survey with close-ended questions) will be more reasonable. Given that we are relatively early in the study of influence pathways, however, open and emergent methods may be a better choice in most near-term cases of research on evaluation influence. That said, a third suggestion is that multiple and mixed methods, both within and across studies of influence, hold considerable appeal.

Fourth, as the concept of pathways suggests, influence is likely to be a dynamic process, playing out over time and involving multiple parties and processes. Methods that trace the sequence of change will be valuable, and single-point-in-time surveys may not capture well the nature of such a dynamic process. Fifth, when thinking about method choices for research on influence and influence pathways, familiar notions such as trade-offs, resources, and pragmatics apply. Thus, thoughtful consideration should be given to what is feasible in a particular piece of research, especially in multisite evaluations where central and site-level end-state influence may be of interest, where influence can be between central and site actors, where evaluation may occur both overall and at the site level, and where diffusion beyond the sites may or may not be of interest. Sixth, as these complexities suggest, investigations with a limited scope may be the wiser choice in the face of limited budget and time frame. To take but one example, elaboration, that is, thinking about evaluation findings in one's own terms, may be a common early step in many evaluation influence pathways. A relatively narrow study of evaluation influence would ask: What circumstances facilitate elaboration and subsequent attitude change or intensity? Seventh, there are several sensible ways to narrow the scope of a study of evaluation influence, either conceptually (for example, by selecting a single influence process or other aspect of pathways) or pragmatically (for example, funders are interested in the influence of a particular evaluation clearinghouse). Eighth, all other things being equal, multisite evaluations may call for narrowing the scope of research on influence to a greater degree than other evaluations (unless more funding is available for investigating the influence of these evaluations). Ninth, studying evaluation influence will often be more challenging than the study of use has been. For example, the more distal influence is from the evaluation, the more challenging it will be to demonstrate the impact of the evaluation. Finally, despite this and other challenges, the study of influence and influence pathways offers considerable promise for better understanding of evaluation and its consequences.

Moving Forward

The world has changed in important ways since the golden age of research on evaluation use. To take but a few salient examples from a U.S. perspective, evaluation has become a routine practice in many organizations; clearinghouses and approved lists are growing in number; the idea of evidence-based practice is commonplace; and the sets of actors and processes that link evaluation to stakeholders and decision makers is more complex, with competing partisans, multiple sources of information, and overlapping policy communities and networks. Recent research that led to the concept of imposed use (Weiss et al., 2005) illustrates the importance of continued research on the consequences of evaluation. More generally, just as the research on evaluation of the 1970s and early 1980s has long helped guide evaluation theory and practice, the promise remains that continued research on evaluation use and influence will pay benefits in years to come.

Support for such research is critical. Sources of funding do exist, at least at times, as illustrated by the NSF research on multisite involvement and use by Lawrenz, King, and colleagues and by a recent initiative at the W. T. Grant Foundation (2009) supporting research on the consequences of research and evaluation. With continued systematic inquiry, as well as the collegial discussion and debate that will accompany it, we should have opportunities for learning. In part, the learning will be about evaluation use and influence, such as better understanding the processes by which evaluation comes to make a difference in varying circumstances. In part, the learning may be about the relative benefits and challenges of a narrower conception of evaluation use in comparison with a broader conception of evaluation influence. In part, the learning may be about influence pathways particular to multisite evaluations. In part, the learning should be about the study of evaluation's consequences itself, with continued experience providing better guidance to subsequent research on evaluation use and influence. And that could be quite influential.

References

Henry, G. T., & Mark, M. M. (2003a). Beyond use: Understanding evaluation's influence on attitudes and actions. *American Journal of Evaluation, 24,* 293–314.

Henry, G. T., & Mark, M. M. (2003b). Toward an agenda for research on evaluation. In C. A. Christie (Ed.), *The practice–theory relationship in evaluation* (pp. 69–80). San Francisco: Jossey-Bass.

Hofstetter, C. H., & Alkin, M. C. (2003). Evaluation use revisited. In T. Kellaghan & D. L. Stufflebeam (Eds.), *International handbook of educational evaluation.* Dordrecht, The Netherlands: Kluwer Academic Press.

House, E., & Howe, K. (1999). *Values in evaluation and social research.* Thousand Oaks, CA: Sage.

Kirkhart, K. (2000). Reconceptualizing evaluation use: An integrated theory of influence. In V. Caracelli & H. Preskill (Eds.), *The expanding scope of evaluation use. New Directions for Evaluation, 88,* 5–24.

Lawrenz, F., Gullickson, A., & Toal, S. (2007). Dissemination: Handmaiden to evaluation use. *American Journal of Evaluation, 28*(3), 275–289.

Leviton, L. C., & Hughes, E. F. X. (1981). Research on the utilization of evaluations: A review and synthesis. *Evaluation Review, 5,* 525–548.

Mark, M. M. (2006). *The consequences of evaluation: Theory, research, and practice.* Presidential address presented at Evaluation 2006: Annual meeting of the American Evaluation Association, Portland, OR.

Mark, M. M. (2009). Credible evidence: Changing the terms of the debate. In S. Donaldson, T. C. Christie, & M. M. Mark (Eds.), *What counts as credible evidence in applied research and evaluation practice?* (pp. 214–238). Thousand Oaks, CA: Sage.

Mark, M. M., & Henry, G. T. (2004). The mechanisms and outcomes of evaluation influence. *Evaluation, 10,* 35–57.

Nutley, S. M., Walter, I., & Davies, H. T. O. (2007). *Using evidence: How research can inform public services.* Bristol, England: Policy Press.

Patton, M. Q. (2008). *Utilization-focused evaluation* (4th ed.). Thousand Oaks, CA: Sage.

Patton, M. Q., Grimes, P. S., Guthrie, K. M., Brennan N. J., French, B. D., & Blyth, D. A. (1977). In search of impact: An analysis of the utilization of federal health evaluation research. In C. H. Weiss (Ed.), *Using social research in public policy making.* Lexington, MA: Lexington Books.

Preskill, H., & Torres, R. (1998). *Evaluative inquiry for organizational learning.* Twin Oaks, CA: Sage.

Weiss, C. H., & Bucavalas, M. J. (1977). The challenge of social research to decision making. In C. H. Weiss (Ed.), *Using social research in public policy making.* Lexington, MA: Lexington Books.

Weiss, C. H., Murphy-Graham, E., & Birkeland, S. (2005). An alternate route to policy influence: How evaluations affect D.A.R.E. *American Journal of Evaluation, 26,* 12–30.

W. T. Grant Foundation. (2009). *RFP for the use of research evidence.* Retrieved from http://www.wtgrantfoundation.org/funding_opportunities/research_grants/rfp_for_the_use_of_research_evidence/use_of_evidence

MELVIN M. MARK is professor and head of Psychology at Penn State University. He has served as president of the American Evaluation Association and as editor of the American Journal of Evaluation.

New Directions for Evaluation • DOI: 10.1002/ev

INDEX

A

Advance Technological Education program. *See* ATE (Advance Technological Education) program

Alkin, M. C., 6, 40, 91, 111

American Educational Research Association, 104

American Evaluation Association (AEA), 77, 103

American Journal of Evaluation, 42

Angermeier, L., 76

Archival review, 3

ATE (Advance Technological Education) program, 9–10

ATE project: background information on, 10–11; citation analysis for, 5, 40–42; end-of-cycle influence visible in, 75; on evaluation involvement, 12; evaluation use illustrated by, 12–13, 109–110; as evaluator-directed program, 80; on implications of an "expected" annual survey, 13–15; involvement cross-case analysis findings on the, 51–57; method used to describe participation, 11; on-line survey/interview data used for, 3–4, 11, 11–13, 12–15, 44–46; organizational culture shaping context of, 77; positive unintended influence reported by, 75; relationship between involvement and use in, 91–93; results-based influence focus on evaluation findings of, 74–75; stakeholder roles in the, 88–89. *See also* Beyond Evaluation Use project cases

B

Balthasar, A., 77

Banilower, E. R., 41

Barnouw, V., 76

Beyond Evaluation Use project cases: citation analysis, 5, 40–42; evaluation use in the, 89–91; examining culture and influence in, 67–68, 73–83; interviews conducted on, 4–5; involvement cross-case analysis of all four, 49–57; relationship between involvement and use in the, 91–93; stakeholder involvement in the, 88–89; time influence visible in life cycle of the, 75; timeline and historical grounding for the, 4*fig*; two on-line surveys conducted, 3–4. *See also* ATE project; CETP project; LSC project; MSP-RET project (Utah State)

Beyond Evaluation Use project (NSF): archival review used during, 3; citation analysis used during, 5, 40–42; culture and influence examined during, 67–68, 73–83; as evaluator-directed program, 80; interviews conducted during, 4–5; origins of the, 1–3; reflections on/lessons learned from the, 59–70; surveys used during the, 3–4; timeline and historical grounding for cases used in, 4*fig*. *See also* National Science Foundation (NSF)

Birkeland, S., 40, 110

Bosma, L., 3

Brandon, P. R., 6, 87, 89, 95

Bucavalas, M. J., 108

Burke, B., 2, 56

C

Callow-Heusser, C., 33, 38, 59, 70, 92

Carlson, B., 104

CETP (Collaboratives for Excellence in Teacher Preparation), 25–26

CETP project: background information on, 26; citation analysis for, 5, 40–42; cultural factors of, 77, 80; evaluation use in the, 89–91, 109–110; findings on involvement, 27–28; history of influence evidenced in, 82, 112–113, 115–116; on implications of voluntary project-level involvement, 30–31; involvement cross-case analysis findings on the, 51–57; on-line survey/interview data used for, 3–4, 27–30, 44–46; positive unintended influence reported by, 75; on project PIs and evaluators use of evaluation, 28–30; relationship between involvement and use in, 91–93; representations of culture in, 78*fig*–79; stakeholder roles in the, 88–89. *See also* Beyond Evaluation Use project cases

Christie, C., 40

Citation analysis, 5, 40–42

Clark, S., 56

Community of practice: annual ITEST PI meeting, 102–103; conference and publication opportunities coordinated by ITEST LRC, 104; ITEST LRC's evaluation technical assistance services for, 99–102; ITEST On-Line Community Web site building, 103–104

Cousins, J. B., 1, 2, 56, 90, 92

Crazy Bull, C., 81

Critical theory, 81

Cultural dimensions: individual perspective, 76; organizational perspective, 76–77; putting culture in context, 77*fig*–78

Cultural factors: avoiding dichotomous thinking about culture, 81; complexities of culture, 77*fig*–78; dimensions of culture, 76–78; evaluator role in raising issues of, 67–69; lessons learned about, 79–81; representations of culture across multisite evaluation, 78*fig*–79; what culture teaches us about influence, 81–82. *See also* Evaluation influence

D

Davies, H.T.O., 108

Dichotomous thinking, 81

DIO (Design-Implementation-Outcomes) cycle, 35, 112

Directorate for Education and Human Resources (EHR), 42

E

Este, D., 78

AMERICAN EVALUATION ASSOCIATION CALL FOR NOMINATIONS

For Editorship of *New Directions for Evaluation*

Term: January 2013 through December 2015
Deadline for Letters of Nomination: August 15, 2011

The American Evaluation Association (AEA) invites nominations for the editorship of *New Directions for Evaluation* (NDE). *New Directions for Evaluation* (NDE), a quarterly sourcebook, is an official publication of the American Evaluation Association. It is a peer-reviewed journal that publishes empirical, methodological, and theoretical works on all aspects of evaluation. The issues may focus on any topic relevant to evaluation as a discipline, profession, or practice. The following illustrate potential foci for NDE:

1. evaluation theory including the philosophical groundings of evaluation or conceptual issues in evaluation. For example, the basis for justifying evaluative con clusions or explications of core concepts like validity;
2. evaluation practice such as approaches, methods, or techniques that can be applied. For example, the use of templates, case studies, or survey research;
3. professional issues of importance for the field of evaluation. For example, the use of evaluation or locus of evaluation capacity;
4. societal issues that draw out the implications of intellectual, social, or cultural developments for the field of evaluation. For example, AIDS, intercultural competence, or poverty.

Editor responsibilities and duties include soliciting proposals for guest edited issues, accepting and rejecting proposals and manuscripts based on their quality and suitability for NDE, guiding issues through the review process, overseeing revisions, and working with the publisher on production matters. The Publisher is responsible for all production aspects of NDE. The Editor will receive modest editorial support of $6,500 per year to cover costs of postage, telephone, photocopying, and other direct expenses. Nominees should meet the following criteria:

- Have a track record of publishing in peer reviewed journals
- Possess good managerial and organizational skills
- Have been a member of AEA for at least 3 years
- Demonstrate a commitment to AEA's values
- Ideally, have previous editorial experience

Self-nominations and nominations of others are welcome. We welcome nominations from individuals and from a pair of colleagues with varied backgrounds who wish to serve as coeditors. Nominees may be asked to submit supplemental materials or to participate in an interview.

Because NDE is a thematic journal, it has an extended lead time between review of a proposal for an issue and publication of an issue. Thus, we are seeking considerable overlap between the current and new editor to allow both for transfer of process knowledge as well as shepherding of issues throughout the process by the new editor that will be published under her or his tutelage.

The deadline for nominations is August 15, 2011. Appointment of the new editor will be made no later than October 15, 2011, so that he or she may meet with the new editor at the 2011 AEA Conference in Anaheim, and learn from the current editor and the journal publisher prior to taking over as editor-in-chief on January 1, 2013.

Send letter of nomination, including curriculum vita, via email to Christina Christie, Chair, AEA NDE Editor Selection Task Force, at tina.christie@ucla.edu. Please feel free to contact Christina with any questions.

NEW DIRECTIONS FOR EVALUATION
ORDER FORM SUBSCRIPTION AND SINGLE ISSUES

DISCOUNTED BACK ISSUES:

Use this form to receive 20% off all back issues of *New Directions for Evaluation*.
All single issues priced at **$23.20** (normally $29.00)

TITLE	ISSUE NO.	ISBN
_____	_____	_____
_____	_____	_____
_____	_____	_____

Call 888-378-2537 or see mailing instructions below. When calling, mention the promotional code JBNND to receive your discount. For a complete list of issues, please visit www.josseybass.com/go/ev

SUBSCRIPTIONS: (1 YEAR, 4 ISSUES)

☐ New Order   ☐ Renewal

U.S.	☐ Individual: $89	☐ Institutional: $271
CANADA/MEXICO	☐ Individual: $89	☐ Institutional: $311
ALL OTHERS	☐ Individual: $113	☐ Institutional: $345

Call 888-378-2537 or see mailing and pricing instructions below.
Online subscriptions are available at www.onlinelibrary.wiley.com

ORDER TOTALS:

Issue / Subscription Amount: $ _____

Shipping Amount: $ _____
(for single issues only – subscription prices include shipping)

Total Amount: $ _____

SHIPPING CHARGES:	
First Item	$5.00
Each Add'l Item	$3.00

(No sales tax for U.S. subscriptions. Canadian residents, add GST for subscription orders. Individual rate subscriptions must be paid by personal check or credit card. Individual rate subscriptions may not be resold as library copies.)

BILLING & SHIPPING INFORMATION:

☐ **PAYMENT ENCLOSED:** *(U.S. check or money order only. All payments must be in U.S. dollars.)*

☐ **CREDIT CARD:**   ☐ VISA   ☐ MC   ☐ AMEX

Card number _____ Exp. Date_____

Card Holder Name_____ Card Issue # _____

Signature _____ Day Phone_____

☐ **BILL ME:** *(U.S. institutional orders only. Purchase order required.)*

Purchase order # _____
Federal Tax ID 13559302 • GST 89102-8052

Name_____

Address_____

Phone_____ E-mail_____

Copy or detach page and send to: **John Wiley & Sons, PTSC, 5th Floor**
989 Market Street, San Francisco, CA 94103-1741

Order Form can also be faxed to: **888-481-2665**

PROMO JBNND